Poetry Explorers 2009

North & East Yorkshire

Edited by Lisa Adlam & Mark Richardson

First published in Great Britain in 2010 by

Young**Writers**

Remus House
Coltsfoot Drive
Peterborough
PE2 9JX
Telephone: 01733 890066
Website: www.youngwriters.co.uk

Foreword

At Young Writers our defining aim is to promote an enjoyment of reading and writing amongst children and young adults. By giving aspiring poets the opportunity to see their work in print, their love of the written word as well as confidence in their own abilities has the chance to blossom.

Our latest competition Poetry Explorers was designed to introduce primary school children to the wonders of creative expression. They were given free reign to write on any theme and in any style, thus encouraging them to use and explore a variety of different poetic forms.

We are proud to present the resulting collection of regional anthologies which are an excellent showcase of young writing talent. With such a diverse range of entries received, the selection process was difficult yet very rewarding. From comical rhymes to poignant verses, there is plenty to entertain and inspire within these pages. We hope you agree that this collection bursting with imagination is one to treasure.

Contents

North & South Cowton Community
Primary School, Northallerton

Nunthorpe Primary School,
Middlesbrough

Rokeby Park Primary School, Hull

St John the Evangelist RC School, Billingham

St Robert's RC Primary School, Harrogate

Sutton Park Primary School, Hull

Wavell Junior School, Catterick Garrison

The Poems

My Magic Box

I have a tin for all my things,
Underneath my bedroom floor.
I put my finger in the crack,
Quietly lift the floorboard back
And there's my store, safely hid,
In a tin with a teddy on top.
A drop of rain from a piece of grass,
Sitting there from a stormy night.
A rainbow with all its colours,
Curved round all my other things.
The first call of a hummingbird,
Singing a beautiful song.
My first friend I ever met
At preschool playing races.
A lock of my first hair,
As soft as cats' fur.
The first dolly I was ever given
By my family on my first birthday.
The first tooth I ever lost
From my gum when I was 6.
A piece of fur from my dog
That is silky and very soft.
I have a tin for all my things,
Underneath my bedroom floor.

Charlotte Kitchen (9)
Anlaby Primary School, Hull

My Magic Box

I have a tin for all my things
Underneath my bedroom floor.
I put my finger in the crack,
Quietly lift the floorboard back
And there's my store safely hid
In a tin with a ted on top.
The first flower from an autumn day,
With the wind blowing the petals away.
The first drop of golden rain
Slowly dropping down the drain.
The first reward I ever took
For doing something good I did.
My first sweet I ever sucked
For doing something good for me.
The third hair from my hamster,
When he was alive that was.
I have a tin for all my things
Underneath my bedroom floor!

Mia Croom (9)
Anlaby Primary School, Hull

The Secret Box

I go in my bedroom
I go under the bed
I put my finger in the crack
Quietly lift back the floorboard
And there's my store
Safely hid in a tin with footballs on the top
My first tooth, gold chipped teeth,
A PSP game,
My first toy and my first football
And there were spiderwebs in it
There is a marble full of dragon smoke.

Joseph Richardson (9)
Anlaby Primary School, Hull

A Tin For All My Things

I have a tin for all my things
Underneath my bedroom floor.
I put my finger to the crack,
Quietly lift back the floorboard
And there's my store safely hid
In a tin with blue feathers on the top.

A huge jar of pear drops
And a sunshine glowing in the dark.
A massive safari park with
Thousands of animals in.
A big scoop of vanilla ice cream
As well I would put a patch of my rabbit's fur.
Also I would put in one of my dog's teeth.

I would keep all of my bad dreams in
And finally a flashing car like fireworks.
I have a tin for all my things
Underneath my bedroom floor.

Katie Murray (9)
Anlaby Primary School, Hull

Secret Tin

I have a tin for all my things
Underneath my bedroom floor
I put my finger in the crack
Quietly lift back the floorboard
And there's my store, safely hid
In a tin with dust caps on the top
A few leather footballs
A marble as big as a dragon's eye
My dog, a snow white puppy
And Bonfire Night.

Callum Wardell (10)
Anlaby Primary School, Hull

The Music I Like

The music I like is
Very special music

At this moment
For instance

I am listening to kids daring
Each other to do big jumps

As a boy grinds
On a rail

And wheels are landing
On the ground

Also a boy skidding
After coming off the biggest ramp

Music, very special music
Just . . . listen.

Oliver Gillyon (9)
Anlaby Primary School, Hull

The Music I Like

The music I like is
Very special music.

At this moment
For instance

I am listening to kids
Daring each other to do high jumps.

As a boy does a wheelie

The boy grinds the
Skateboard along the pole.

Music, very special music.
Just listen . . .

Joshua Omond (9)
Anlaby Primary School, Hull

Treasure Box

I have a tin for all of my things,
Underneath my bedroom floor.
I put my finger in the crack,
I quietly lifted the floorboards back.
There's my store
Safely hidden in a tin with skateboards on the top.
A stone that I found on the beach,
A smaller tin in the bigger tin with all my money in,
A dragon tooth which is very sharp.
Some old food from my hamster,
A stack of some Spanish money,
A glass of colourful sweets,
And a toy truck as big as
The Empire State building.
I have a tin for all of my things
Underneath my bedroom floor.

Jack Emanuel (9)
Anlaby Primary School, Hull

The Mary Celeste

When we arrived at school that day
The computers were still running
But there were no pupils
In the classroom
There wasn't a single teacher
In one of the rooms, we found abandoned books
Everyone had seemed to vanish
We also found
Two half-empty lunchboxes
Three open literacy books
Some think the children were kidnapped
Others say they turned into ghosts
Me, I think they all flew away with magic wings
'Any more fairies?'

Lennon Kemp (9)
Anlaby Primary School, Hull

YoungWriters

The Mary Celeste

When we arrived in school that day,
The computers were running,
But there were no pupils in the classroom,
There wasn't a single person in school,
In one of the rooms we found two pieces of work undone,
Jumpers lay on tables
And a pack lunch half-eaten.
Everyone seemed to have disappeared just like a flick.
We also found a packet of salt and vinegar crisps on the chair
And others say they have been captured
By Mega Pixel 3 thousand aliens,
Others say by a builder.
Me, I think that they flew away into the sky
With Mr Cornwall shouting, 'Any more fairies?'

Demieleigh Nicola Skinner (10)
Anlaby Primary School, Hull

The Secret Box

When we arrived at school that day
The computers were still running
There were no children in classroom,
There wasn't a single whisper,
In one of the rooms we found a half-finished sum,
Everyone seemed to have vanished.
We also found ten smelly, dusty shoes,
Three pieces of ripped work
And a lunchbox containing berries,
A packet of chips and a ham sandwich.
Some think the children were zombies,
The others say man-eating builders barged from across the way
And swallowed them with their tea.

Thomas Sugden (10)
Anlaby Primary School, Hull

Untitled

When we arrived at the school that day,
The computers were still running,
But there were no children in the classrooms.
There wasn't a single person,
In one of the rooms we found an unfinished sum,
Everyone seemed to vanish.
We also found two school bags,
Three cups of tea
And a lunchbox containing an orange,
A ham sandwich and a packet of cheese and onion crisps.
Some think the children were taken by goblins,
Others say man-eating builders barged from across the way
And swallowed them with their tea.

Kienan Walker (9)
Anlaby Primary School, Hull

Treasure Box

I have a tin for all my things underneath my bedroom floor
I put my finger in the crack quietly
Lift back the floorboards and there's my store
Safely hid in a tin with lilies on the top
I put in my box snowflakes that sparkle like a diamond
My gran's necklace, a pearl from a very fine clam
I put in my box a whisker from the cutest kitten
And a water fairy
I will put in my box my favourite book,
My first wish and my friends.

Laura Payne (9)
Anlaby Primary School, Hull

I Like The Music

The music I like is very special music
At this moment for instance
I'm listening to KCFM
Talking on the radio
My dog eating
Munching her food
And as Taylor shouts at Mum
And as the washing machine spins around
Music, very special music, just listen.

Connor Morgan-Hanson (9)
Anlaby Primary School, Hull

I Have A Tin For All My Things

Underneath my bedroom floor
I put my finger in the crack,
Quietly lift back the floorboard
And there's my store safely hid
In a tin with dragons on the top.
A few old teeth with a mood ring.

It is a toffee colour which looks like butterscotch sauce
With red, black and blue.

Lois Amity Beaumont (10)
Anlaby Primary School, Hull

Sky Diving

When the doors opened I felt a brush of wind in my face.
I finally dived out in the majestic wind and shot through the clouds.
The sound was so loud I could barely hear myself speak.
I pulled the string for my parachute handle
And then I went very slowly and there was a little breeze.
I gently floated through the clouds.
I could see the ground.
Now I saw where I had to land and I safely floated to the bottom.

Owen Drury (9)
Anlaby Primary School, Hull

Music I Like

At this moment for instance
I am listening to crickets
Rubbing their legs together
As the wind echoes in my ears
As the surf rolls in on the waves
And the crackling of a BBQ
And the tent rustles in the wind
Music, very special music, just listen.

Ethan Jay Straker (9)
Anlaby Primary School, Hull

The Music I Like

The music I like is very special music.
At this moment for instance I am listening to Guns N' Roses
Playing on TV and my hamster is drinking,
Rattling his water bottles
And as my brother plays his guitar
The kettle boils,
Music, very special music, just listen.

Harry Storr (10)
Anlaby Primary School, Hull

9

The Mountain And The Climber

The mountain wept as the climber
Stuck his pickaxe in the rockface.

The mountain roared in anger,
Sending rocks tumbling down
Into the bottomless ravine.

The climber struck back with a burst of energy,
By stabbing his studded boot
In the crevice making the mountain cry out in pain.

The mountain cried out loud sending
Gushes of water down the mountainside
Making the climber lose his grip.

He was hanging on by one axe.
He was slowly sliding down sending a deep
Cut in the side of the mountain.

The mountain coughed causing a
Snowstorm and gale force winds
Around the mountain.

The mountain went quiet,
He thought the climber had gone,
Suddenly he appeared,
He had reached the top,
The mountain had lost.

James Widgery (11)
Bootham Junior School, York

The Night

It was a starry night.
The stars were glittering, shining, twinkling,
Whirling, swirling, screaming.
They were winking at me.

It was a dark night.
The moon was glowing, shining, twinkling,
Coughing.
It was talking to me.

It was a moon lit night.
The sky was dark, spooky, scary, some dark
Flowing black hair.
The sky was looking at me.

It was a windy night.
The wind coughed, spluttered, wailed, cried,
Winced.
The wind whistled for me.

A starry night, a dark night, a moonlight night,
A windy night.
The world loves me!

Emily Smith (10)
Bootham Junior School, York

The Hill

The hill was asleep, no heart, no soul, just empty.
It stood still just watching over time and air.
The green hair that it grew swayed in the wind.
It started to wake up.
It was foggy on it.
It started to rain on it.
There was a howling gale washing over the hill.
It had woken up, but then came the sun
And flowers grew and the hill was asleep.

James Alderson Edwards (11)
Bootham Junior School, York

The Car And The Weather

The car roared into action
The rain began to crash down
The car wasn't going to give up
It roared, screeched and bellowed
As it sprinted through the motorway

But then . . .

The rain splattered, coughed
And finally stopped
The car came out of the rain
But hail struck with force

But suddenly . . .

The hail shouted, screamed
And at the end stopped
Then the car came out of the hail
The thunder roared with fear
And gathered all its energy

But immediately . . .

The car was nowhere to be seen.

Jan Janeczek (11)
Bootham Junior School, York

The Cloud And The Rain

The wet rain tried to run through the cloud.
The fluffy cloud sucked up all the water.

They travelled past fields,
Mountains and ocean too.

They were lost!
The cloud got angry.
The cloud picked up the rain.
Then he threw it down covering the Earth.

William Dean (10)
Bootham Junior School, York

The Tornado

The wind blew up a mighty brew.
Rain, sleet and hail too.
All mixed in to make . . .
A noisy tornado, big mistake,
The rampaging tornado struck through town,
Wheezing, whirling up and down.
Suddenly snow flops to the ground,
Bouncing snow makes such a sweet sound.
Inside the tornado snow makes it cough,
The snow that falls is very soft.
The tornado fought back,
Like trains on a track.
The snow fought back hard
And was winning by a yard
But then spluttered snow stopped to a halt
And then the snow turned into salt,
Went into the tornado, couldn't stop,
The tornado whirled and frightfully flopped.
Tornado defeated, snow had won
Only twelve months for winter to come.

Alexander Goldthorpe (10)
Bootham Junior School, York

Battle Between Sun And Cloud

The cloud pushed hard at the sun and laughed in his face.
The sun bounced back and dived through the cloud's cheek.
The cloud shivered with fear and a tear fell from his face.
The water he cried came down as rain.
The rain jumped and laughed as it hit the ground.
People ran for shelter.
But the sun became friends with the cloud,
The rain stopped and saved it for another day.

Amelia Lawrence-Downs (10)
Bootham Junior School, York

The Tractor

Coughing and spluttering
The tractor goes by
Smoking his pipe
The tractor goes by.

Past the combine harvester
Chugging by
Huffing and chugging
Puffing by.

It's dark now
Noise in the air
Thunder shouting
Snow is falling all around
Rain is sleeping on the ground.

The digger throwing mud around
Digging and throwing
Jumping up and down.

George Avery (10)
Bootham Junior School, York

The Battle Of The Tornado And The Sun

The tornado lashed out at the sun,
The sun twisted round and dodged the vicious attack,
The tornado threw houses at the sun.
The sun had had enough,
He leaped at the tornado,
The tornado looked at the sun and ate him in one,
There was a still silence for a while,
Then the sun pushed out of the side of the tornado,
The tornado winced
And plummeted towards the Earth and disintegrated,
Down on the Earth the ashes of the tornado were scattering around.

Robert Ingram (10)
Bootham Junior School, York

14

The Hurricane Vs Tornado

The hurricane,
The bully of all weather,
Buildings huddle close together,
Palm trees bend and sway.

The hurricane,
A swirling, whirling mass of vapour,
Wind and rain.

The tornado
Twizzles like a turkey twizzler.
It roars and screams.
Inferior storms cry and moan.

The tornado
Like a spinning top,
Terror, chaos.

James Nelson (10)
Bootham Junior School, York

The Weather Battle

The thunder roared,
The lightning flashed,
The wind blew hard,
The sun screamed, 'I'm scared!'

The hail sprinted down,
The snow ran after the hail,
The rain soaked everything,
The sun screamed, 'I'm scared!'

Suddenly the sun shone
As bright as it could,
Then everything stopped
And all went silent.

Supreet Kaur (10)
Bootham Junior School, York

Volcano

The volcano coughed over the forest,
Roaring and dancing, it threw rocks out.
It shook and grew, destroying the land,
Fire blew out from deep inside.

Suddenly it calmed and stopped,
Snow slept all over it,
It slept for years through sun and rain.

People started climbing on his back,
He got angry and cried.
Tears were lava, the rocks were punching fists,
Then suddenly it stopped and slept.

Charles Corner (10)
Bootham Junior School, York

The Meteor And The Wind

The meteor pushed the wind out of its way,
'You can't stop me no way, no way,'
But the wind knocked the meteor back
Into the moon with a deafening crack,
The moon awoke in such a rage,
He blew those fools right away
And to this day the meteor was banished to outer space.

Alexander Riches (10)
Bootham Junior School, York

Battle Between Weathers

The sun pushed the snow away.
The snow fell silently to the ground and ran away.
Next came the wind.
He puffed up his cheeks and blocked out the sun.
Next came the rain which bounced on the ground.
The sun crept up the wetness.
The ground was dry again.

Tilly-Mae James (10)
Bootham Junior School, York

Sun And Ice

The sun sat on the ice melting it.
The ice cried, making steam rise and forcing the sun back.
The sun sneaked up behind the melted ice
And made it evaporate.
The evaporated ice took a running jump
And fell back down onto the sun as snow.
Then the sun went out and the world was destroyed.

Charlotte Kelsall (10)
Bootham Junior School, York

The Battle

The truck growled at the combine harvester
Then they charged.
The combine barged the truck.
They stared at each other.
The truck glared and the combine hissed.
The truck dodged and the combine coughed
And when the day was done, they both went into the shed.

James Gilbert (10)
Bootham Junior School, York

The Snow In December

The snow danced as it fell to the ground
Making a large patch of white.
It was the most beautiful patch of snow in the field.
The snow fluttered its eyelashes.
Then a raincloud came by, it cried on the snow.
The snow ran away and came back on another December's day.

Phoebe King (10)
Bootham Junior School, York

My Mum

Coins clink,
Boys nash,
People munch,
Cars crash,
Wines pour,
Gamblers cheat,
Mums shout, 'Eat, eat.'

Snakes hiss,
Guns shoot,
Queens scream,
Trains toot,
Rockets zoom,
Dogs growl,
Mum refs, 'Foul, foul.'

Teachers shout,
Clocks tick,
Lions roar,
Pens click,
Hyenas laugh,
Old men crouch,
Mum hurts, 'Ouch, ouch.'

Caleb Carlton-King (10)
Derwent Junior School, York

Magic Of The Brain

Such a sight I saw,
I saw a puppy curled up in its basket,
It was so cute,
Its ears just dangled there down beside its face
And it looked so glossy as if it had been painted with varnish,
It made me feel lively but cheerful
And playful at the same time,
Such a sight I saw.

Tillymae Whitehead (10)
Derwent Junior School, York

Ears Hear (Classroom Noise)

Chairs scrape
Pencils tap
Roofs slam
Rulers rap
Papers rip
Teachers talk
Pupils stamp, walk! Walk!

Chelsea Hope (11)
Derwent Junior School, York

Such Great Stuff

Such great stuff for me
I see old and new stuff
I see big and small stuff
I see great and boring stuff
I see old and new friends
But most of all
I hear laughter that never ends.

Rhiannon Wheatland (9)
Derwent Junior School, York

This Week I Will . . .

On Monday I will listen to what people have to say.
On Tuesday I will touch, touch and feel all day.
On Wednesday I will speak, say and only speak.
On Thursday I will see, see, look and peek.
On Friday I will smell, smell all the lovely scents!

Bethany Mae Chambers (9)
Derwent Junior School, York

It's Autumn

The glistening skin of cracking conkers like a sword just cleaned.
The bronze covering lives in a hedgehog-like shield,
Just like we live in houses.
Then get bigger, bigger and bigger through the year,
Then you know it's autumn.

There's a blazing bonfire overhead, with a screaming stash inside.
From its lair comes flying smoke that was once many
crunchy leaves.
Its body spreads through the dale,
Then you know it's autumn.

As the leaves start to fall from trees they turn brown and die.
They fall one by one, never in a crowd.
Yet together they lie in a communal grave and rot,
Then you know it's autumn.

Joshua Crabtree (9)
Glaisdale CP School, Whitby

Brambles

Brilliant brambles glisten in the sun.
Beautiful brambles stain your clothes.
Big brambles grow in the bush.
Black brambles are witches' favourite fruit.

Hamish Miller (7)
Glaisdale CP School, Whitby

Is It Really Autumn?

I see leaves fall down to earth.
Watch them as they twist, turn and flutter.
Brown to gold and orange to red.
I see beautiful black brambles glisten in the bright shining sun.
Watch them as they increase their size . . . juicy . . . flawless
And perfect . . . brilliant.
I smell smoke from home garden bonfires.
The smell gathers around me to tell me it's autumn.
I smell sweet nectar from flowers all around.
Busy bees work and work for a great reward.
I hear birds getting ready for migration
Calling for communication. Ready . . . set . . . go!

I sense the bareness of silent hogweed
As it whispers goodbye to its fellow friends.

Charlotte Benn (10)
Glaisdale CP School, Whitby

Autumn Wonders

Apples, sweet, crunchy and red,
Descending to the cold, hard earth below,
Begin their wait to rot and give their seeds to the ground.

Brambles turn a beautiful jet-black
Painting your mouth a brilliant purple every single time you chew.

Conkers, bronze and hard as granite
Plummet down to the ground from the great horse chestnut,
Then hide, like the most expensive truffle in the world.

Leaves turn a golden brown
Loosen themselves and drift from the tree.

These are just some of the great wonders of autumn
That everyone should treasure.

Alasdair Miller (9)
Glaisdale CP School, Whitby

It's The End Of Summer

Cracking conkers leave their old mother to start anew.
Black sweet brambles are picked to be digested.

Through the evergreen churchyard grass starts to die.
In the dale leaves wither from the trees.
Over the moors green bracken starts to turn gold, to rust,
Brown to dust.
Time starts to slow.
The wind gets stronger.
Days get shorter.
Nights get longer.
Farmers gather their harvest.
Flowers breathe no more.
Summer has ended.

Jordan Todd (9)
Glaisdale CP School, Whitby

In Autumn

In autumn, you can pick the
brambles after they've all grown.

In autumn you can see the large
bronze moon as it hangs low in the sky.

In autumn you can listen to the leaves rustle in the wind,
while they shiver and turn.

In autumn you can taste the smoky
air in the dark night.

In autumn you can watch the conkers fly down from the trees
their leaves flapping like birds' wings.

Megan Lees (9)
Glaisdale CP School, Whitby

Migration

If I was a bird flying south for the winter sun,
I would let the breeze flow through my feathers.

If I was a bird flying south for the winter sun,
I would be the head of the group and fly like the wind.

If I was a bird flying south for the winter sun,
I would dance through the sky like a ballerina in a tutu.

If I was a bird flying south for the winter sun,
I would share my talent by singing my saddest song.

Alex Lloyd (11)
Glaisdale CP School, Whitby

Awesome Autumn

Breaking bark
Burning bonfires
Cracking conkers
Red rowan
Swooping swallow
Dying dandelions
Wild wind
Sighing sun
Winter is on its way.

Ruby Elliott (7)
Glaisdale CP School, Whitby

Golden Leaf

Like a twinkling star in the autumn sky,
Slowly turning cartwheels.
It breathes in the air,
Then lands on the soft, smooth grass.
The golden conker leaf
Crumbles in the glistening sunshine.

Joe Lees (8)
Glaisdale CP School, Whitby

Autumn

Old leaves,
Gold leaves,
Flying leaves,
Dying leaves,
Twirling leaves,
Swirling leaves,
Red leaves,
Dead leaves.

Mia Ferns (7)
Glaisdale CP School, Whitby

Remember The Foxglove

Remember the foxglove when it was purple?
Remember the foxglove when it was tall?
Remember the foxglove when it swayed in the summer breeze?
Remember the foxglove when it was lovely?
Look at the foxglove now,
A brown, crisp spike,
Its beauty has gone.

Anna Lees (7)
Glaisdale CP School, Whitby

Autumn Is Here

Black brambles grow protected by prickles
Which scrape and scratch the picker.

Beautiful brambles will stain your
Fingers if you squash them.

Big brambles are lovely to eat
Sharing them with my grandma.

Ryan Spedding (7)
Glaisdale CP School, Whitby

Hull Fair

Merry-go-round
I am the merry-go-round
I'll spin until you're sick
You'll get very dizzy
Us horses will give you a kick
We are very busy
I am the merry-go-round!

The twister
Behold I am the twister
I'll do more than make you sick
I will grab you with my arms but *ooo!* I just miss you!
You'll want to get off in a tick
Behold I am the twister.

Conrad Moy (10)
Hall Road Primary School, Hull

Hull Fair

I can see the big wheel with enormous lights
That are as bright as the sun.
I can see the scary ghost train
With ghosts as white as snow
That is whiter and brighter than white.
I can hear people screaming
As loud as 52 roaring lions.
I can hear them screaming because of the ghost train
With the scary Frankenstein.
I can smell sweet candyfloss
That floats through the sky.

Kerrie Knight (7)
Hall Road Primary School, Hull

Hull Fair

I can see the
Gigantic, enormous, big wheel moving about very slowly
With lights as shiny stars.

I can hear
Girls screaming as loud as a lion roaring in a jungle
Full with animals.

I can smell
Juicy hot dogs floating across my face
And hot mouth-watering candyfloss
And hot dogs sizzling in the pan.

Shannon Gartshore (7)
Hall Road Primary School, Hull

Hull Fair

I can see the gigantic rides
And their bright, shiny lights shining
Like stars in the sky.

I can hear people screaming
Like three lions roaring like thunder
In the pitch-black sky.

I can smell mouth-watering juicy hot dogs
And burgers.

Sherrieleigh Bass (7)
Hall Road Primary School, Hull

Hull Fair

I can see the gigantic ghost train with the ghosts
Lights shining like the stars in the sky
I can hear the people screaming
As loud as a tiger.

Tereza Grannon (8)
Hall Road Primary School, Hull

Hull Fair

I can smell the mouth-watering beefburgers
Sizzling in the steaming hot frying pan
And the sweet, juicy, soft candyfloss
And the spicy, lovely hot dog frying in the frying pan.
I can see the enormous rides
And I can see the lights shining off the rides.
I can hear the screaming as loud as a jet
And the loud music like a thunderstorm.

Kieran Bowers (7)
Hall Road Primary School, Hull

Hull Fair

I can see rides flashing like thunder
And a bungee jump with kids in.

I can hear music as loud as a disco.
I can hear rides as loud as thunder.

I can smell candyfloss in the stalls.
I can smell mouth-watering hot dogs
Like a dog eating sausages

Sophia Smart-Lee (7)
Hall Road Primary School, Hull

Hull Fair

Hull Fair
I can see the bright lights.
I can hear loud music.
I can smell juicy hot dogs.
I feel very scared.
I can see bumper cars.
I can hear screaming.

Emma Moxon (7)
Hall Road Primary School, Hull

Monster Called Twister

There's some monsters at Hull fair,
One of them is called Twister,
With its four arms twisting everywhere,
Waving to people to come.
He's quite a good monster,
He picks people up and spins them around,
To have fun only for one pound!

Marta Ribeiro (10)
Hall Road Primary School, Hull

Hull Fair

I can see the enormous bouncing frog,
It is a big, huge spring.

I can hear enormous motors roaring as loud as thunder
And a very huge lion roaring.

I can smell mouth-watering, delicious hot dogs sizzling in a pan.
Hot dogs are big long rainbow stripes.

Luke Mostyn (7)
Hall Road Primary School, Hull

Hull Fair

I can see a gigantic bungee jump
As big as the school.

I can hear loud music,
It is as loud as a lion.

I can smell greasy drizzling hot dogs
That are hot as a fire.

Reesha Phillipson (7)
Hall Road Primary School, Hull

Hull Fair

I can see the big wheel spinning, twizzling, whizzing
And whirling around really fast.
It is as fast as a cheetah running.

I can hear music as loud as a lion roaring at its loudest.
I can hear screaming as loud as a tiger.

Callum Dailly (7)
Hall Road Primary School, Hull

Hull Fair

I can see the big wheel.
I can hear some people screaming.
I can smell mouth-watering hot dogs.
I feel excited because it is fun.
I can see a train speeding past.

Shouq Alrashed (7)
Hall Road Primary School, Hull

Hull Fair

I can see the creepy ghost train with ghosts hanging down like snow.
I can see toads hopping around.
I can hear screaming as loud as thunder in the pitch-black sky.
I can smell juicy mouth-watering hot dogs in the sizzling hot pan.

Andrea Lacken (8)
Hall Road Primary School, Hull

Hull Fair

I can see the giant helicopter round the sky.
I can smell mouth-watering,
Very hot hot dogs.
I feel very lovely.

Charline Andrews (7)
Hall Road Primary School, Hull

Hull Fair

I can see the exciting rides.
I can hear noises and screaming.
I can smell the beautiful hot dogs.
I feel excited and happy.

Dannielle Holmes (7)
Hall Road Primary School, Hull

Hull Fair

I can see the big wheel as big as a giant.
I can smell dazzling hot dogs in my mouth at Hull fair.
I feel excited because there are so many rides
That I don't know which to go on.

Bradley Moy (7)
Hall Road Primary School, Hull

Hull Fair

I can see gigantic rides going up and down.
I hear screaming as loud as thunder.
I can smell mouth-watering hot dogs in the air.

Etaine Bowmer (6)
Hall Road Primary School, Hull

I Am Here

I can smell the hot heavenly hot dogs, my mouth is watering
I can smell the delicious dinky doughnuts, give me more
I can smell the chunky, cheesy chips, they're stuck together
I can see the flashing lights flash, flash, flash
I can see the rides moving, wow I'm going on that
I can see the people on the rides, I love Yarm Fair
I can hear music blaring in my ear on all the rides
I can hear people screaming loudly and happily
I can hear the rides screeching, what a terrible noise
I can touch the sticky toffee apples, gooey
I can touch the curly candyfloss melting in my hand
I can touch the bars of the rides, I love it
I can taste the juicy pork burgers, my favourite food
I can taste the heavenly hot dogs with the melted butter
I can taste the delicious dinky doughnuts just been cooked.

I love Yarm Fair.

Neve Watts (9)
Junction Farm Primary School, Stockton-on-Tees

I Can Smell And See

I can smell lovely hot dogs.
I can smell toffee apples.
I can smell smoke coming from the waltzers.
I can hear people screaming.

Callum Basham (8)
Junction Farm Primary School, Stockton-on-Tees

The Fair At Yarm

T he fair is a really good place
H ot dogs always in my tum
E veryone's happy

F lying hot dogs flying around
A ll the people are happy on rides
I ce cold weather all around
R eally fun rides on the ground

A t the fair all the slides
T ime goes by all the time

Y arm Farm is a really good fair
A ll the rides are really good
R ides are really scary, some are not
M y friends are always there, or not.

Jade Starkey (8)
Junction Farm Primary School, Stockton-on-Tees

Fantastic Fair

F antastic fair
A beautiful roller coaster going speeding fast
N o people eating nothing
T oo good for nobody to be there
A lovely hot dog lying in the hot dog stand
S o good for nobody can resist
T all roller coasters so high
I could go on the sticky wall all day
C an you go so high?

F unny fortune tellers
A ir whizzing through your head
I ce cold weather
R ides making Yarm Fair beautiful.

Matthew Cooney (8)
Junction Farm Primary School, Stockton-on-Tees

Fairgrounds

F unny, fabulous rides bouncing up and down
A bsolutely beautiful lights all around
I cky candy apples, red and juicy
R iding on rides with my friend Lucy
G orgeous candyfloss
R ides going off
O h my, rides make you sick
U ncool, brothers are only six
N ever is there a boring ride
D rum down the big slide
S o you'll be sad when you leave but you'll never be brave.

Abigail Swales (8)
Junction Farm Primary School, Stockton-on-Tees

At The Fair

A ll the food in my tummy,
T he rides are too scary for me without my mummy.

T he rides are so funny,
H ow much money?
E gyptian weather, so, so sunny.

F antastic food all around,
A lways making lots of sound,
I rritating teenagers who are very loud,
R ides, rides, rides all go round!

Sophie Shepherd (8)
Junction Farm Primary School, Stockton-on-Tees

Yarm Fair's Today

Y ummy hot dogs yummy and scrummy.
A t the fair, all good rides with my mummy.
R olling rides all so good.
M oving rides make a thud.

F antastic fun, food and all.
A ll the rides are so tall.
I 'm here now making some noise.
R ough, hook-a-duck, winning toys.
S unny day, bite of cold just I'm here now, now, now!

Ellie Coleman (8)
Junction Farm Primary School, Stockton-on-Tees

Yarm Fair

Y ummy hot dogs
A t the stand
R eally fast rides
M agic turns

F antastic day we're going home
A t long last
I n the UK now it's a
R ainy day.

Nathan John Carter (8)
Junction Farm Primary School, Stockton-on-Tees

Yarm Fair

I can smell . . .
I can smell the sizzling sausages in a black pan.
I can smell the sizzling sweet sweets.

I can see . . .
I can see the tallest ride in the city.
I can see the big shops in the distance where I'm standing.

Niamh Stephanie Hawes (9)
Junction Farm Primary School, Stockton-on-Tees

34

Yarm Fair

Y ummy candyfloss waiting for a home in your belly
A mazing massive rides taking up your view of the sky
R ides making you faint they're that high
M assive rides making you look.

F un as can be, come back to Yarm
A hot dog begging you to eat it
I cy cold weather taking up your scream
R ides making your hair stand on end.

Joshua Mahmood (8)
Junction Farm Primary School, Stockton-on-Tees

Yarm Fair

Y ummy candyfloss crackling on my tongue
A lovely sausage in my bun
R ed ketchup in my tum
M y mum, I'm telling her come, come, come

F luffy floss in the shops
A lovely apple that doesn't flop
I wanted more rides, I agitated my mum
R ain in the sky and we're done.

Joe Howe (8)
Junction Farm Primary School, Stockton-on-Tees

Funfair

F ear is here.
U nder and over speed goes.
N ow everyone's having fun.
F air is here.
A speed is spinning.
I n Yarm, people will be having fun.
R ides run everywhere.

Emily Stewart-Titchiner (8)
Junction Farm Primary School, Stockton-on-Tees

Go To Yarm

Y arm Fair is so cool, I'm on the Crazy Frog!
A ll the people are loving it.
R ides bouncing up and down.
M y candy cane is gorgeous and so is yours.

F airs are so cool there should be one every day.
A ll my friends are here.
I 'll have some chips now.
R ides are so rusty but I still love them.

Megan McCullagh (8)
Junction Farm Primary School, Stockton-on-Tees

Cuddly Teddy

Cuddly teddy is sleepy
He likes to cuddle into the pillows
He likes to get cuddled by a human
Cuddly teddy is sleepy
He likes to cuddle into the pillows
He likes to get cuddled by a human
Cuddly teddy is sleepy
He likes to cuddle into the pillows.

Cameron Arnett (7)
Junction Farm Primary School, Stockton-on-Tees

Gingerbread Man

You can see their smile.
They have a thin body.
Sometimes they can be very crumbly.
On it, it has Smartie eyes.
They stare at you in the shops.
They are nice to eat.
When you eat them we go yummy!

Joseph Smith (8)
Junction Farm Primary School, Stockton-on-Tees

Yarm Fair

I loved the delicious hot dogs going round and round my mouth.
I loved all the amazing spinning rides.
I loved the sugary candyfloss.
I like seeing people screaming on the fantastic rides.
I loved screaming on the creepy ghost ride.
I loved playing hook-a-duck and winning a lovely teddy bear.
I loved having fun on the Higgledy Piggledy House.
I love Yarm Fair, I'm here, crowded, around people having fun.

James Green (8)
Junction Farm Primary School, Stockton-on-Tees

Gingerbread Man

Lovely, crunchy biscuit, yummy in my tummy.
Gingerbread down your throat,
Gingery taste in your mouth.
Your mum comes back from the bakers
And a gingerbread man is there for after tea.
You bite into and *crunch, crunch.*

Joel Wylie (7)
Junction Farm Primary School, Stockton-on-Tees

Silence

It looks like lovely creamy white milk.
It reminds me of a very strict teacher telling her class to shhh!
It sounds like nothing, just silence in the air.
It smells like fresh clean water dripping from the tap.
The colour is black, as cold as the night.
Last but not least, it feels like relaxing in the warm summer sun
And it feels so snuggly in my hot cosy bed. *Zzzzzzzz.*

Ellie Olivia Gould (8)
Kirk Hammerton CE Primary School, York

Sadness

Rain dripping on the roof,
Sounds like sadness.

Feeling like your heart is breaking in two,
Sadness is a burst of surprise,
Like when somebody says boo.

Reminding me of my stolen phone,
Sadness is the sorrow of my life.

Sadness smells of the Christmas pudding,
Burning in the oven.

A girl sitting alone is what sadness looks like.

Beatrice Townsend (10)
Kirk Hammerton CE Primary School, York

Silence

Every sound has been taken away
It's left us only darkness and silence

The sweet apple pie cooking in the kitchen
And the piano keys sitting still in the back of the room

It feels like aliens have taken away the world
It reminds me of the days of war.

Tom Hooper (10)
Kirk Hammerton CE Primary School, York

Fun

Jolly friends working happily together
In the sun friends laughing joyfully
Happiness of people going out together
Me and my dog playing nicely
And the golden glazing sun.

William Backhouse (9)
Kirk Hammerton CE Primary School, York

Anger

Anger is as black as a midnight sky,
Anger is red in the face,
A broken heart is what anger feels like,
Anger reminds me of trees blowing in the wind,
Anger smells of smoke,
Rushing water is the sound of anger.

Katherine Hooper (9)
Kirk Hammerton CE Primary School, York

Happiness

It reminds you of fun times.
Happiness smells like there's going to be fun.
It's the colour of a rainbow.
It looks like fun.
It gives you a good feeling.
It sounds amazing.

Elliott Green (8)
Kirk Hammerton CE Primary School, York

Sadness

Sadness is the sound of heartbroken music.
Sadness smells of the beautiful smell of roses.
Sadness feels like nobody's there.
Sadness is the colour of the blue sky.
Sadness looks like everything bad is happening.
Sadness reminds you of everything bad.

Chloe Guy Jobbling (8)
Kirk Hammerton CE Primary School, York

Happiness

It reminds people of happy times.
It smells like tasty sweets.
Happiness looks like a funfair.
Happiness is the colour of a rainbow.
Happiness sounds like happy things are going to happen.
It feels like a rainbow has opened inside of you.

Jonathan Richardson (8)
Kirk Hammerton CE Primary School, York

What Do Vampires Do When It's Not Hallowe'en

What do vampires do when it's not Hallowe'en?
They could be very keen
To come to your dull bedroom to suck your blood,
To suck your blood good.

What do vampires do when it's not Hallowe'en?
They could go to school,
They could swim in a swimming pool full of blood,
Or jump in the pool with a thud.

What do vampires do when it's not Hallowe'en?
When they're wearing a cloak,
They disappear in a cloud of smoke,
And you start to choke.

What do vampires do when it's not Hallowe'en?
Are they nice amiable people?
Do they comb their barbed wire-like hair?
The vampires take good care.

What do vampires do when it's not Hallowe'en?
Their teeth could get repaired,
So look out humans *get prepared*
The vampires are coming to *scare*.

Paul Foster-Daniells (10)
Linton-on-Ouse Primary School, York

The Diving Board

My legs were shaking,
I was dripping wet.
Would I mess up?
Would I hit my head?

I walked to the ladder,
Put my hand on the bar,
I was amazed with myself,
That I'd got this far.

I climbed up one step,
Put my foot on step two,
I was so scared,
My legs turned to goo.

But I gritted my teeth,
And kept on going,
But when I got to the top
I started moaning.

I can't do it, I thought.
'Yes you can,' I said.
I walked to the edge,
My stomach felt like lead.

A plummeting drop,
Into deep, dark blue,
For the second time
My legs felt like goo.

But then I jumped!
In a wonderful freefall,
I hit the water,
Gave my friends a call:

'I like it,' I shouted. I was happy.
I've done it, I thought. Just me!

Jacob Speiran (10)
Linton-on-Ouse Primary School, York

The Grim Reaper

After Hallowe'en the jobs are never finished.
Terror here, terror there,
The Reaper has some jobs to do . . .
Terror here, terror there,
He sharpens his pickaxe ready to chop,
Terror here, terror there,
Washing his robes and dyeing them black.
Terror here, terror there,
Cleaning his jars to store souls in.
Terror here, terror there,
Making a map to show where he's going.
Terror here, terror there,
Goes to the skeleton store to buy illness.
Terror here, terror there,
Repairing his broken bones for next time.
Terror here, terror there,
He practises looking scarier.
Terror here, terror there.
Cutting his lawn with his sharpened scythe . . .
So you see the Reaper is never bored
In his dark,
Dark cave.

Robert Garner (10)
Linton-on-Ouse Primary School, York

Penguin

Brave diver
Belly flopper
Baby saver
Enemy fighter
Ice skater
Fin clapper
Pebble lover.

Toyah Potter (8)
Linton-on-Ouse Primary School, York

What Do Dragons Do When It's Not Hallowe'en?

What do dragons do when it's not Hallowe'en?
What do dragons do when it's not Hallowe'en?
What do dragons do? What do dragons do?
What do dragons, what do dragons,
What do dragons do?

Do they polish their fangs, hanging like boomerangs?
Do they sharpen their horns by which lives are torn?

Do they guard their eggs with their spiky spiked tail?
Do they curl round their treasure with great, great pleasure?

Do they breathe fire at ghosts all pale and white?
Do they get into a great big dragon fight?

Do they hunt at night to give us all a fright?
Do they fly by night in the moonlight?

What do dragons do when it's not Hallowe'en?
What do dragons do when it's not Hallowe'en?
What do dragons do? What do dragons do?
What do dragons, what do dragons,
What do dragons do?

Nathan Burroughs (10)
Linton-on-Ouse Primary School, York

Whales

People swallower
Wave maker
Super splasher
Tail stander
Land hater
Ship crusher.

Hannah Walton-Hughes (8)
Linton-on-Ouse Primary School, York

What Does A Dragon Do When It's Not Hallowe'en?

On the side of the volcano the fearsome dragon sleeps.
Always waiting . . .
Waiting for some treats!
One eye open, he searches for his prey,
But he needs to eat princesses every single day.
For him, a knight is never enough.
But when he's defeated them he blows a smoke ring . . .
Puff!
He cleans his fangs and puts his contact lenses in,
And then he puts his tutu on and has a dance and sing!
On the side of the volcano the fearsome dragon sleeps.
Always waiting . . .
Waiting for some treats!

Eleanor Richardson (10)
Linton-on-Ouse Primary School, York

David

My big brother has a funny hat collection,
He would win in any hat inspection.
He has:
Funny hats,
Bunny hats,
Singing happy birthday hats.
Donkey hats,
Monkey hats,
All kind of animal hats.
Small hats,
Tall hats,
All the days of the week hats.
My big brother David has a funny hat collection,
He would win in any hat inspection!

Emily Garner (10)
Linton-on-Ouse Primary School, York

Porpoise

Sea splasher
Bubble maker
Food taker
Fun creator
Fin clapper
Water drinker
Sea jumper
Race winner
Air breather
Super leaper.

Rebekah Hall (8)
Linton-on-Ouse Primary School, York

Pear

I'm a pear
Without any hair.
You can eat me
And squash me.
But I won't care.
But don't you dare
Toss me in the air.
It doesn't matter.
What a clatter.
Just leave me in a splatter.

Gage Andrews (7)
Linton-on-Ouse Primary School, York

Dolphin

Wave jumper
People lover
Joy bringer
Smashing swimmer
Fish eater.

Chloe Adgo (8)
Linton-on-Ouse Primary School, York

Turtle

Super swimmer
Speed breaker
Rubbish collector
Silly sleeper
Various hunter.

Holly Menzies (8)
Linton-on-Ouse Primary School, York

What Am I Not

I'm not a boy who likes writing.
I'm not a boy who likes homework.
I'm not a boy who likes comprehension.
I'm not a boy who dislikes football.
I'm not a boy who dislikes cricket.
I'm not a boy who dislikes rugby.
What I like and dislike is still yet to be confirmed,
But all I can say
Is I like to play
All the time
In fact - all day
So I don't know why I'm writing this poem
If I don't like writing
I don't know what I'm doing!

Edward Greaves (10)
Long Marston CE Primary School, York

Ladies

Thin ladies,
Fat ladies,
Tall ladies,
Small ladies,
Rude ladies,
Nude ladies,
Crude ladies,
Ladies.

Yellow ladies,
Red ladies,
Blue ladies,
Green ladies,
Pink ladies,
Purple ladies,
Black ladies,
Ladies.

Scary ladies,
Happy ladies,
Sad ladies,
Mad ladies,
Flirting ladies,
Dirty ladies,
Crazy ladies,
Ladies.

Stripy ladies,
Splodgy ladies,
Podgy ladies,
Curly ladies,
Straight ladies,
Wiggly ladies,
Ladies.

Karolina Milciukaite (10)
Long Marston CE Primary School, York

A-Z Of Animals

A is for atrocious ants
B is for barging buffalos
C is for cute cats
D is for dancing ducks
E is for eating elephants
F is for frantic fish
G is for great golden eagles
H is for horrible hippos
I is for ignorant iguanas
J is for jumping jaguars
K is for kicking kangaroos
L is for leaping lemurs
M is for magic monkeys
N is for naughty newts
O is for orange octopuses
P is for peaceful pandas
Q is for quirky quails
R is for ravenous rabbits
S is for slimy salamanders
T is for terrifying tarantulas
U is for unknown uakaris
V is for vicious vultures
W is for wavy wolves
X is for extraordinary X-ray fish
Y is for yummy yaks
Z is for zany zebras.

Tom Adams (10)
Long Marston CE Primary School, York

Please Don't Touch The Elephant!

Here lies the body of Charlotte Le-Gant,
Hung up in the air,
By an angry elephant.

She wanted to touch it,
To feel its skin,
But it wasn't happy,
It made a great din.

So, using its trunk
And all of its might,
It picked up her throat,
Till she was out of sight.

It choked her and poked her and
Killed her quite dead,
Then dropped her right down,
Onto her head.

The service was short,
There was no laughter,
Everyone was waiting,
For the party after!

Adam Brown (10)
Long Marston CE Primary School, York

A Sense Of Pain

Pain looks like a scrunched face of an old man dying.
Pain sounds like a terrible scream of a fearful man being eaten alive.
Pain feels like a cold wall on an icy day.
Pain tastes like captured stale air from a dingy cobwebbed tomb.
Pain smells like the rotting stench of a carcass on a
                                        hot summer's day.

Rhys Meredith (10)
Long Marston CE Primary School, York

A Sense Of Hopes

Hope looks like a big smile on a newborn baby
In its newly bought cot.

Hope feels like a warm hug for orphan children
From a stranger.

Hope sounds like big applause in assembly
On Friday afternoon.

Hope tastes like a big, fat, cheesy pizza
On a Saturday in front of the TV watching X Factor.

Hope smells like a vase of roses
On a winter's afternoon
In the freshly polished room.

Holly Wilson & Eddy Telford (10)
Long Marston CE Primary School, York

A Farming Year

January to April sheep have their lambs whilst the rams have a rest.
Come July it is time for the lambs to come off their mums,
For the sheep do not have any more bruises on their tums.
From July onwards lambs are weighed and off to market.
During June and July, farmers give a tip whilst they clip.
In August the farmers bale, whilst the children find a trail.
Through September farmers pick potatoes
And the children tiptoe in the night.
In October farmers put tup raddle on whilst the children tell tales.
All through November and December they get the cows in
Whilst the sows have their piglets.

Thomas Farrar (9)
Long Marston CE Primary School, York

My Magic Box

(Based on 'Magic Box' by Kit Wright)

I will put in my box . . .
The laugh of a laughing lion
The scaly tail of a singing mermaid
A singing seagull sitting on a house.

I will put in my box . . .
A Jaffa Cake with a broken heart
A thunderous night at a Haven holiday
A Chinese whisper from the reddest dragon.

I will put in my box . . .
The smell of a scented corn dolly filling the house
A swish of a silk dress filling the room
The last words of an uncle and the first word of a baby

I will go on my box . . .
Through the rushing rapids of Richmond River
Over the steep drop of Niagara Falls
Walking the length of the Great Wall of China.

Megan Brown (10)
Lynnfield CP School, Hartlepool

Friends

F reddie's great at football
R azzak's great at kicking the ball
I an's great at typing on the computer
E manuel's great at writing stories
N orman's great at PE
D eclan's great at numeracy
S tephen's great at poetry

These are all my friends.

Aaron Metcalfe (10)
Lynnfield CP School, Hartlepool

I Will Put In My Box

(Based on 'Magic Box' by Kit Wright)

I will put in my box . . .
The blowing of a winter night
The twittering of a bird in the blue sky above
The beating of a true love's heart.

I will put in my box . . .
The blinking of a tropical fish
The mane of a tiger and the stripes of a lion
The popping of a pen and the point of a bubble.

I will go with my box . . .
Through the rushing waves of the Caspian Sea
And through the blazing hot desert
To the frozen wastes of the Antarctic.

I will decorate my box with
The shining stars in the corners
A rose in the centre surrounded by the love of God.

Georgia Hamilton (10)
Lynnfield CP School, Hartlepool

Football

Football, football is a game with a ball.
Wherever you go you'll see a football.
Bangladesh, Russia maybe even Ukraine.
Wherever you go, football is insane.
Your dream is to play for a football team.
You may be confident but people might boo you!
You think you've won, you think the game's done,
But what if they come back, you might get the sack!

Ahmed Muftady (10)
Lynnfield CP School, Hartlepool

Shooting Star

Shooting star
Burning bright
In the middle
Of the night, night, night.
Zooming through
The galaxy
On your way
To me, me, me, me.
I'll wish a wish
Before you die
And tumble down
The starry sky
That once again
One magic night
I might see you
Burning bright . . .

Shamima Aktha Uddin (7)
Lynnfield CP School, Hartlepool

When I Lost My Boot

One day I went to pick a fruit
But I lost my boot.
My boot had a bow on it.
Three minutes ago
I remember.
It was stuck in my basketball hoop!
So I finished my soup.
Then I looked in my friend's pocket,
His name was Koop,
He had one but that was a paper boot.
Then we jumped and jumped and jumped,
At last
I got back my boot.

Haleema Durrani (8)
Lynnfield CP School, Hartlepool

Ghost In The Castle

The ghost in the castle
Clank, clank, clank
Vanishes in front of you
And makes you go weak.

The ghost in the castle
Squeak, boing, bang
Is a knight in armour
Who clanks and clangs.

The ghost in the castle
Groan, groan, groan
Is a poor old king
Placed in his throne.

Rachel Skinner (8)
Lynnfield CP School, Hartlepool

Flowers In The Garden

Red like cherry tomatoes
Blue like the summer sky
Green like juicy sweet grapes
Yellow like the sun
Purple like beetroot in a pan
Pink like a big flamingo

I like flowers.

Courtney Lynn (7)
Lynnfield CP School, Hartlepool

Bonfire Night

On Bonfire Night, families gather to watch the beautiful sight,
Bang! An explosion of colours shooting high into the night sky
Many wild colours, more than you imagine, fill the sky.

Shujath Syed (9)
Lynnfield CP School, Hartlepool

A Gnome Poem

I am a gnome
Sitting at home
All alone
Writing this poem
Sitting all by myself
On the garden shed shelf
I wish, I wish, I wish I was an elf!

Ryan Bartram (7)
Lynnfield CP School, Hartlepool

Brush Every Day

Brush every day, sends the decay away.
Brush in the morning, Dad's warning.
Brush after meals, gives a healthy smile.
Brush at night, gives the decay a fright
And if you floss, your teeth will gloss.
But after you brush use polish
And people will be astonished.

Mufshana Yasmin (8)
Lynnfield CP School, Hartlepool

My Dog Ate The Postman

I have a little dog and her name is Jessie.
Her favourite place to sleep is anywhere that's neat
But her favourite thing to eat
Is our postman Pete!
We went outside, to our surprise
She had eaten him head to toe!

Heather Currell (9)
Lynnfield CP School, Hartlepool

Miss Frankland

Miss Frankland, from my school is so kind,
Taking interest in our scabs, she doesn't mind
Blood or bits of skin gone green
And tenderly, she smoothes on cream.
Miss Frankland says, 'Shall I ring up Mum or Dad?
I think that cut looks very bad.'

Anika Molik (8)
Lynnfield CP School, Hartlepool

Volcanoes

Volcanoes are explosive and very, very *big!*
Volcanoes spit out fire!
Volcanoes are silent.
Volcanoes are loud.

Volcanoes are deadly so stay away!

Sara Razzaq (10)
Lynnfield CP School, Hartlepool

Sweet Cutie

What can I say? Hip hip hooray
Sitting down
As I lay
Looking at people that I see
But they're not as pretty as you and me.

Nicole Hastings (10)
Lynnfield CP School, Hartlepool

Stars

S tars, oh stars, they're so very bright
T hey're so shiny and such a sight
A s they shine in the astonishing night
R eversing in and out of the sky
S tars are so magical and shine in the night.

Nujha Begum (10)
Lynnfield CP School, Hartlepool

Hallowe'en

At Hallowe'en I dressed up
Blue and green as a wicked wizard,
I went around the corner and a boy said boo!
I went to a party and it was cool,
I went trick or treating, then I got freaked out.

Shatil Syed (7)
Lynnfield CP School, Hartlepool

When A Tornado Came To Get Me!

I woke up one night and I had a fright!
I saw a cone swirling in the snow,
Oh *wait!* It was a tornado,
It was my dad's drill, drilling through the earth,
As it sneezed in my ear it *really hurt!*
The tornado is candyfloss melting in my mouth,
I just wish it could pass and go south,
Whirling, swirling and spinning in the air,
It called out my name and kicked down our garden chair.
Bash!
It was like a duck's beak coming to eat me,
Because it had already destroyed my house and tree,
I went downstairs and got harassed,
But before I knew it, the tornado has passed!

Lucy Maitland (9)
Newbald Primary School, North Newbald

Snow

The snow is a melting figure,
Not seen every week,
As I nibble my chestnut which is bigger
Than a hot chocolate cup leak.

Like a sprinkle of dust,
The snow falls like nothing before,
The white stuff never rests
With everyone asking for more!

It is as cold as the coldest ice cream
With people shivering all around me
And chestnut trees rustling near the stream
As I'm sat behind the frozen sea!

When I play around in the snow
Which is from the -10°C cold sky
And is white, sparkling, glittery, gluey snow,
When I'm watching the snowballs fly.

But the snow is now done here in this town
It has left us feeling cool,
Then everyone started to sadly frown,
When the snow left us a frozen pool!

Joseph Singleton (10)
Newbald Primary School, North Newbald

The Tale Of My Dog

At home I have a hairy dog
She's brown and white and as solid as a log
Her ears are huge and her eyes are bright
Her teeth are sharp but she would not bite!
Her favourite game is playing with her snake
She pulls it like a rope and gives it a shake
She's my best friend so loyal and true
She is known to me as *Missy-Moo*.

Reece Wild (9)
Newbald Primary School, North Newbald

Winner

The Tornado

As the tornado started to appear,
It whistled and whispered into my ear.

The wind blew into my hair,
Then candyfloss was made in thin air.

The tornado flew in the sky,
It went ever so very high.

The tornado was like a giant nail,
Hammering into the earth, it would never fail.

The tornado smiled and spun around,
It was so loud I was drowned in sound.

The tornado was my dad's drill,
Destroying the city, winning one nil!

The tornado is a monster that eats up trees,
It was as chaotic as a giant sneeze.

The tornado was like a washing machine,
But it didn't get close to make this city clean.

The tornado was finished, his job was done,
He's demolished the city, he's had his fun!

Ben Watson (10)
Newbald Primary School, North Newbald

My Parrots

My parrots are blue and green,
They are a boy and a girl.
Their names are: Paco and Rico.
They are nice and they are playing,
They eat fresh fruits and seeds.
They make noises like a whistle.
I like my parrots!

Andreea Voinea (9)
Newbald Primary School, North Newbald

I Love The Rain

The rain is my sprinkler in my back garden.
It also makes a sound and that is the tiptoe of mice
Dancing in the loft.
And when I always went up there it always made me cough.
The other thing it sounded like was a mini waterfall
Trickling down a mountain.
That always made me think of a large chocolate fountain.
I love the rain, it's my favourite weather
And I always find a black or white feather.
Dewy gardens, dewy hedge, rain dripping off the window ledge.
But all amongst the garden seeds my soggy boots with soggy heels
They were obviously left out in the rain,
Oh no! they're wet, oh, not again.
Hang on, I hear something, something strange,
Was it the trees or the breeze.
No hang on a minute, I think I know, it is the raindrops saying hello.
As I'm walking back to my house the sound my boots make are
splish, splash, splosh.
As I'm walking I say bye-bye
And that was followed by a big long sigh.

Jemima Philip (9)
Newbald Primary School, North Newbald

My Kitten

His purr is as loud as an engine's tick
And his teeth are as sharp as knives.
His tail is as thin as a French fry
And as pointy as a needle.
His claw is an axe digging in my skin
And his ears are the Eiffel Tower.
His eyes are as bright as a torch at night.
His whiskers are like pipe cleaners
And his fur is as soft as a velvet rug.
This playful little bundle is my kitten!

Bethany Sheard (9)
Newbald Primary School, North Newbald

60

The Weather

The thunder came crashing
And flashing over the hill,

Crash, crackly
Crash, crackly.

The thunder slams like a big door,
Run and hide on the floor!

Here it comes again,
The angry thunder,

Bang, bash
Bang, bash.

The thunder and lightning looks
Like a tree root in the sky.

The thunder like a sharp blade
So the thunder had fun.

Fran Tomlinson (9)
Newbald Primary School, North Newbald

My Littlest Dog

My sweet little dog, he's a Rottweiler you know.
When I see him in the morning, my face begins to glow.

He's only one year old but despite this, he is very big and bold.
He has a black and brown thick coat
That keeps him from getting cold.

He likes to chew our hands and feet,
But we still love him, he's so sweet.

He likes to go out for walks and play
Then sleeps like a baby for the rest of the day.

Alfie, Alfie we all love you like mad.
When you are not with me, I'm very sad.

Charlotte Messer (8)
Newbald Primary School, North Newbald

Thunder And Lightning

The thunder was as loud as my little sister.
Crash, bang!
The lightning was as loud as my friends running down the street.
The smashing of thunder was as loud as the clock's
Tick-tock!
The flashing of lightning is as bright as the sun.
Thunder is as loud as the cracking of paper.
Crack!
Lightning was as bright as the biggest light.
Thunder is the root of a tree.
The lightning is us with a Christmas cracker.
Crack, crash
The lightning is a disco ball.
The thunder is a table being crushed.

Amy Tooke (9)
Newbald Primary School, North Newbald

Joy As A Feeling

What does it feel like?
Happiness.
What colour is it?
Red.
What does it remind me of?
Christmas.
What does it taste like?
Chips and fish.
What does it sound like?
Squealing.
What does it smell like?
Turkey.
What does it look like?
Christmas trees.

Oliver Ellis (8)
Newbald Primary School, North Newbald

Turbo

His name is Turbo,
He is cuddly and tubby.

Perhaps that's all the treats he eats!
When he is on his wheel, he is like a speed machine.

He is as fast as a racing car,
But he doesn't go far.

He makes me laugh like a hyena,
When he runs around the room.

He is my special pet, my own
Little hamster, my mate Turbo.

Conor Smith (10)
Newbald Primary School, North Newbald

Shep

His heart pumps like lightning
And his bark is very frightening.

He's like a panda, black and white
And when annoyed he likes to fight.

He is a dog with very floppy ears
And he's 11 but in a dog's world, he is 77 years.

He likes to have walks
And he is a dog that talks.

As a result his gnashers are like crocodile teeth
And he is a dog that belongs to Grandad Keith.

Joseph Morton (9)
Newbald Primary School, North Newbald

Thunder And Lightning

The thunder was stomping like a giant around the world.
The thunder sounds like the Wombles stamping about
As they failed their driving test.

The loud thunder sounded like a gun firing.
Bang!

As somebody was opening beans, the thunder came down
And scared the trees.
The lightning struck
Like a massive explosion.

Fiona Shearsmith (9)
Newbald Primary School, North Newbald

My Poem Called Surprise

Surprise smells of my birthday cake.
Surprise reminds me of my baby sister starting to talk.
Surprise makes me look happy.
Surprise makes me feel like dancing.
Surprise tastes like Christmas pudding.
Surprise makes me think of the colour red.
Surprise sounds like music.

Emily Green (8)
Newbald Primary School, North Newbald

My Sadness Poem

Sadness feels like my team losing.
Sadness is blue, it's the colour of tears.
Sadness tastes like fear.
Sadness looks like someone crying in the darkness.
Sadness reminds me of being bullied and hurt.
Sadness is like an animal's tears.
Sadness is the feeling of loneliness!

Ryan Askem (8)
Newbald Primary School, North Newbald

Joy

Joy is the smell of Christmas dinner.
Joy is white for the snow falling in December.
Joy sounds like bells jingling as Santa flies by your house.
Joy is loads of presents in my lounge.
Joy is being really warm.
Joy reminds me of cracking Christmas crackers.
Joy tastes like hot and sticky Christmas pudding.

Jack Sheard (8)
Newbald Primary School, North Newbald

Terror!

Terror is the vicious attack of a big, hungry lion.
Terror is being eaten by a nasty dinosaur.
Terror feels like being scared in the dark.
The colour of terror is red.
Terror smells like hot chilli sauce.
Terror looks like a dragon.
Terror tastes like hot fried chicken.

Charles Duxbury (8)
Newbald Primary School, North Newbald

The Pain!

Pain reminds me of getting hurt by a lion.
The colour of pain is red, the colour of blood.
Pain tastes like hot food.
Pain smells like steam.
Pain is a lion running after you.
Pain sounds like a tiger growling.
Pain feels like crying.

Joshua Robinson (7)
Newbald Primary School, North Newbald

My Cats Are As Fast As Cheetahs

My cats are as fast as cheetahs.
They can jump as high as mountains.
Their claws are like knives and their teeth are like daggers.
They sleep all day and eat all night.
Their fur is as soft as silk and is shiny as stars
And they have eyes as wide as oceans.

Evie Tomlinson (9)
Newbald Primary School, North Newbald

Love

Love reminds me of Christmas.
Love sounds like me opening my presents.
Love tastes like chocolate pudding.
Love looks like a spiky Christmas tree.
Love is all the colours of the rainbow.
Love smells of Yorkshire pudding!

Evie Wilson (6)
Newbald Primary School, North Newbald

The Feeling Of Pain!

Pain feels like hitting my head on the hard, wooden table.
Pain is red for blood when you cut your knee.
Pain smells of the lush, green grass on the muddy football field.
Pain reminds me of cracking my head open on the pavement.
Pain sounds of me screaming and yelling for my mum.
Pain tastes like the blood in my mouth when my tooth has fallen out.

Lucas Wilson (8)
Newbald Primary School, North Newbald

Happiness And Sadness

Happiness, happiness up a tree.
Happiness, happiness inside me.
Happiness, happiness inside you.
Happiness, happiness gone down cold.
Sadness, sadness, it's coming to me.
Sadness, sadness, it's going to you.

James Mitchell (7)
Newbald Primary School, North Newbald

Wonder

Wonder is the bright lights at Hull Fair.
Wonder is the delicious burgers and the hot dogs.
Wonder is the colour of sparkly gold.
Wonder feels like sticky toffee apples.
Wonder tastes like eating junk food.

Charlotte Kelly (8)
Newbald Primary School, North Newbald

Happiness

Happiness smells like Hallowe'en cake.
It reminds me of Hallowe'en.
Happiness is green like the ghosts and black like the witch's cat.
It makes the sound, *oh, oh, oh, oh, ooh.*
Happiness looks like other people trick or treating.

Heather Holmes (7)
Newbald Primary School, North Newbald

Underwater

In the water, in the waves
Seals splashing through the sea.
In the sea cave lives a shark with sharp teeth.
Manta ray flying underwater.
Seaweed slimy and green.
Fish darting around me.
Dolphins swimming gracefully,
Rock pools with crabs in them.
Clownfish giggling and telling jokes.
Crabs inviting me for tea.
The sun shining on the sea making it glimmer.
If you go there today
The sea horses are bound not to come and play.

Ellie Garbutt (8)
North & South Cowton Community Primary School, Northallerton

Under The Sea

Shoals of fish, swimming gracefully
Through the sparkling blue water.
Darting around like hundreds of torpedoes.

Sea horses swaying like long, green seaweed.

Golden sand, like multicoloured diamonds
Shimmering in the light of the ocean.

Dripping wet sea caves filled with silver crystals.

Fish speeding through the beautiful coral
Like brightly coloured cars,
Zooming through an underwater city.

Carl Hughes (10)
North & South Cowton Community Primary School, Northallerton

Space

Blast-off!
The spaceship went up with a trail of fire,
In seconds surrounded by darkness and glowing stars.
The moon was white and shining, with dark craters,
Finally we made it to Mars.
We jumped out and explored,
There was a voice behind us.
I turned around and saw another spaceman.
My ship had broken thrusters,
Help!
We took the spaceman back and were named heroes.

Matthew Clark (8)
North & South Cowton Community Primary School, Northallerton

Haunted House

Cold, dark, eerie.
Silent, dusty, grey.
The rooms are all deserted,
No one ever comes this way.
There are lots of broken objects
And a scary oak front door.
Nobody comes here anymore,
Except ghouls, ghosts and devils.

And all because of ancient lore,
This is the *haunted house.*

Rachel Hannah Elphick (9)
North & South Cowton Community Primary School, Northallerton

Rainforest

Tall trees touching the sky in giant canopies,
Pounding waterfalls swirling on to racing rivers,
Shoals of tiny angelfish gather upstream,
Buzzing insects flitting here and there,
Miniature parrots gliding through the green leaves,
Giant woolly rats scuttling across the leaf litter,
Long green snakes disguising themselves as elongated vines,
A sound of unknown animals sends shivers up my spine.

Jack Walmsley (10)
North & South Cowton Community Primary School, Northallerton

The Great Sea Adventure

Set sail for the seven seas.
Sails billowing in the wind.
The boat is called the Football King.
Seeing all the cool sights in the sea.
Dolphins, sharks, fish and jellyfish,
Millions of them never been seen.
Boats sinking, people swimming for their lives.
People making friends, having fun.

John William Clark (9)
North & South Cowton Community Primary School, Northallerton

Volcano

Ash spreading like big grey moths,
Dark brown bark hanging from toasted trees,
Spitting rock rolling down the jagged slope,
River of fire bubbling and sizzling,
Flames shooting high in the sky.

Lewis Wilson (8)
North & South Cowton Community Primary School, Northallerton

The Blitz

Screaming, shrieking, sky droning, distant whining,
A deadly echo as I bolt to shelter from the blazing bombs.
Acrid smoke, like a grey life-taking blanket,
A stinking, gagging inferno gives no mercy.
Clouds of billowing brick dust descend like a desert sandstorm,
Dry in my mouth, flickering flames burning more
Than my tongue can stand.
Raging and roaring, bomb after bomb, taking street after street
And life after life.
Helplessly sprinting, there is no escape from the smouldering rubble
Which tears my feet, making my skin red-raw and flaky.

This is only the beginning.

Evie Kerr (10)
Nunthorpe Primary School, Middlesbrough

Fish Poem

Fishes, some scaly, small, big or tall.
Happily they swim in the sea with their family.
Sharks some blue, black or white,
But be careful, they bite.
Orange, hard, strong, the crab scuttles along the seabed.
Pointy, comes in many colours and sizes,
The starfish lies as still as a statue under the water.
As beautiful as a star that has fallen out of the sky.
Dolphins, friendly and very intelligent
And they leap out of the water so very high.
Turtle, a big green turtle,
Pushing itself through the water, not very fast but fascinating.

Oliver Wildmore (8)
Nunthorpe Primary School, Middlesbrough

Blitz

Dark, dingy skies groaned ferociously
Like a hungry tiger in echoing streets.
I could see fierce, ferocious flames glowing prominently
From the distance as if they wanted children.
Rough, rugged rocks and splintered stones cut my feet
Like a sharp silver sword.
Choking acrid smoke filled my mouth and poisoned my lungs
Like it wanted to kill me.
The reeking stench of ash filled my nose as I climb over rubble
Searching for my family.
What will happen next?

Hannah Stevenson (11)
Nunthorpe Primary School, Middlesbrough

Egypt

They weren't waking for 60 years.
In the hot sun.
Made a pyramid out of sand or stone.
They made six cows wake.
They grow crops.
They killed dogs and cats.
They eat old bread.
They found Tutankhamun.
The found a door.
They are the dead mummies.

Eleanor Vassallo (7)
Nunthorpe Primary School, Middlesbrough

The Life Of A Slave

It's hard work being a slave.
You have to be quick.
You have to be brave.
Some work high.
Some work low.
Slaves' lives are full of woe.
Some of us die.
Some of us don't.
Some of us regret it
But some of us won't.

Harry Harland (7)
Nunthorpe Primary School, Middlesbrough

The Blitz

I staggered through the unwelcoming home feeling the faint,
Sharp wallpaper, my sore hand began to peel.
Smoky air enters my dry, empty mouth as I cough heavily.
Seeing the deadly, damp street as I make my way through
The rusty, broken door.
Hearing the horrifying sound of screaming, whining,
Freezing cold babies wishing for their mum.
As the burning stench creeps up my nose
I feel my head bang like a drum.
Could this get any worse?

Megan Charlotte Porley (10)
Nunthorpe Primary School, Middlesbrough

The Midnight Fox

The furry fox is as black as a juicy sloe berry.
Softly, silently, the blackberry fox glares.
Sharp, shiny teeth rip through her prey.
Sneakily, gracefully, the fox creeps through the colossal wood.

Maisie Henderson (9)
Nunthorpe Primary School, Middlesbrough

Blitz

Balls of heat, burning, bouncing balls of heat
Travelling down from the shadowy sky.
The acrid burning, choking smell of smoke filled my throat
With acrid gas and was suffocating me.
The sharp shards of glass stick through my aching bloody feet.
The bombs screech and also scream
Like people dying in houses on flames.
The terrifying taste of poisonous smoke spreading
All around the rubble filled street.
The war has began.

Kai Lucas Beattie (11)
Nunthorpe Primary School, Middlesbrough

Mr And Mrs Colour

Mr Red bumped his head on the bed.
Mr Brown met a clown in the town.
Mr Black had a big sack.
Mr Yellow was a great fellow.
Mr Green has been seen being mean.
Mrs Pink fell down the sink getting a drink.
Mrs White had a fright during the night.
Mrs Grey had to pay for a sack of hay.
Mrs Plum put her thumb through a drum.
Mrs Blue bought something new.

Thomas Hetherington (7)
Nunthorpe Primary School, Middlesbrough

The Midnight Fox

The fox's fur is as dark as a starless night.
Quietly, quickly she creaks, carefully to her prey.
Her eyes are green glow sticks in a pitch dark night.
Sneakily, she watches her prey, like a tiger.

Jonathan Wetherley (9)
Nunthorpe Primary School, Middlesbrough

The Midnight Fox

The fox silent, careful, stares down at its prey.
Eyes as sharp as a knife.
Gracefully, silently she clambers over the slippery rocks.
The ebony fox is as elegant as a cat.
The moonlit fur compliments her fierce, green eyes.
The fox barks as if to call her children.
The long, curled tail is covered with soft, silky fur.
The body is dry ink coated with polish.
It is an unforgettable, mysterious midnight fox.

Katie Kellerman (9)
Nunthorpe Primary School, Middlesbrough

Blitz

As I rushed over to the shelter almost tripping over the lifeless,
Leafless garden, a bomb exploded.
Feeling the long wild grass then finally touched the rigid metal
Of the old shelter.
Smelling tar on the road melting
And catching my nose's attention the air was smoky and ashy.
Bouncing, blazing, furious dark, gloomy skies filled with droning
Sounds of planes and loud whining of bombs crashing down.
Confusion now takes over the world.

Adrian Cole (10)
Nunthorpe Primary School, Middlesbrough

Blitz

There is a horrible smell like pure blood
And even worse there was a taste like burning in my throat.
I touched terrible smoke even though I was scared,
They were crying more than me, they were petrified.
All I could see in the sky was bomb after bomb.
I can't believe, I'm still alive.

Daniel Mallett (10)
Nunthorpe Primary School, Middlesbrough

Blitz

As I wander the destroyed streets I see
German planes flying, dropping bombs on us.
Lying down on my bed I hear the roaring of bombs crashing down
And setting homes alight.
Thundering balls of fire race along the sooty streets.
Gasping for air ashy tastes fill my mouth instantly.
Reaching out I feel the ashy air around me.
Bombs land instantly trapping us in an unsafe environment.
What a tragic start to life.

Elizabeth Vassallo (10)
Nunthorpe Primary School, Middlesbrough

Blitz

Bouncing, glowing skies shake like a threatening, roaring lion.
Hot burning old wood as I touch the texture
of old crumpled wallpaper.
The clogging stench of burning, deadly roaring fire
fills my lungs as I run.
The drowning sound of screams and whines
echoed down the crumpled street.
The deadly taste of acrid smoke clogs my lungs as I'm going.
Will the war ever end?

Gabrielle Nicole Ahmed (11)
Nunthorpe Primary School, Middlesbrough

A Fish Tale

The red spotty fish wiggled and waggled along the deep blue sea.
He was worried and lost without his friends, where could they be?
He searched nearly everywhere but his friends he could not see.
He said, 'If I don't find them soon, it will be time for my tea.'
Red saw some bubbles and swam to check behind a rock.
Guess where his friends were hiding? In a smelly old sock!

Mia Gibson (7)
Nunthorpe Primary School, Middlesbrough

Blitz

Blazing bombs explode in the bellowing street of people yelling
And panicking.
Blazing fireballs echo into the midnight crisis of the war.
The last touch of our house goes up into flames.
As ashy smoke starts to burn in my mouth I have to spit it out.
My head spins like a wheel in the confusion.
As the sky explodes with anger it is as if it is talking to me.

Is this the *end*?

Sophie Taylor (10)
Nunthorpe Primary School, Middlesbrough

Blitz

Bomb after bomb ruining life after life and home after home.
Deafening drones of bombers scare London's folk.
The sky explodes and moans with furious rage and anger.
Fireballs explode and bright illuminate the midnight sky
As planes fight.
Acrid smoke suffocates and clogs my lungs and takes life after life.
Bombs shatter glass and break wooden doors that are flesh.
I fear that more are on the way.

Jake Goode (10)
Nunthorpe Primary School, Middlesbrough

The Midnight Fox

The fox's coat was black as the midnight sky
And her teeth as sharp as blades.

Her eyes are glittering stars.
Quietly, stealthily the fox ambushed its prey.

Elegantly and carefully she carried her prize
Back to her den.

Jack Brown, Luke Robert Vickers, James Stephenson (9),
Holly Boyce (10), & Emma Rogers
Nunthorpe Primary School, Middlesbrough

The Midnight Fox

The rare fox's jet coat is as black as a witch's cat.
She smiles as her tail sways in the air
like a ship's sail blowing in the wind.
Secretly, the fox catches its prey.
Eyes as green as grass.
Sparkling, smooth, the fox carefully cleans her fur.
Gracefully as a ballet dancer the fox sprints back to its den.
Sneaky, speedy.

Ruby Mason (9)
Nunthorpe Primary School, Middlesbrough

Pyramid Poem

Hot,
Dry, stony,
Boiling, big,
Pointy, steep,
Gigantic, yellow,
High, tall, small, dusty,
Sandy, massive, hard, soft.

Hannah Rounsley-Freer (8)
Nunthorpe Primary School, Middlesbrough

Tomb Of A Pharaoh

Pyramids can be large or small,
Made from stone and sandstone.
Home of the Egyptian kings who once lived and roamed.
Now guarded by ancient traps unknown
Hidden in the sand of the pyramids
The treasure inside could be sold but because of their mummies
who might try to scare those who enter were not told.

Taylor Williams (7)
Nunthorpe Primary School, Middlesbrough

Blitz

Screaming, smoke penetrated my throat like a bloody knife.
Glowing, gushy smoke flew furiously over the city.
Poisonous fumes swirled around
Like a race that's turned out of control.
Choking cries leapt out of my house like a tiger in a cage.
Thousands of splinters leap on my arm as I try to sprint away.
Will it ever end?

Callum Markie (10)
Nunthorpe Primary School, Middlesbrough

The Midnight Fox

The fox is as black as an inky sloe berry.
Sneakily she watches her prey.
Her fur is as black as ravens' feathers.
Her nose is an inky, starless night.
Her teeth are sharp blades.
Quietly, stealthily taking prey to her den.
Her watchful eyes are as radiant as fresh snow.

Ryan Willoughby (9)
Nunthorpe Primary School, Middlesbrough

Blitz

Bombs falling mercilessly,
Killing everyone in their way.
The taste of ash fills the air.
The choking scent of death chases me as I run down the street.
The raging sky roars in anger.
I can feel the rubble as it tumbles on top of me.
It is just the beginning.

Ciaran Malcolm (11)
Nunthorpe Primary School, Middlesbrough

Autumn

A corns are falling off trees.
U mbrellas up, people rushing in the rain.
T rees turn rusty while leaves are blowing down.
U nder piles of colourful leaves - watch out,
    there's a hedgehog about!
M isty mornings – don't want to get up.
N ights are drawing in.

Emily Wilson (7)
Nunthorpe Primary School, Middlesbrough

The Midnight Fox

The coat was black as the midnight sky
And her teeth as sharp as blades.

Her eyes glittering like stars.
Quietly, stealthily, the fox ambushed its prey.

Elegantly and sweetly she carried her prize,
Back to her den.

James Dokubo (9)
Nunthorpe Primary School, Middlesbrough

The Midnight Fox

The fox is a racing cheetah,
Sprinting after its prey,
Sneakily it gallops to its cub,
The cub, a curious cute ball of fluff,
Her fur is as shiny as a moonlit sky,
Strong and calm she runs back to her den.

Dion Jade Watts (9)
Nunthorpe Primary School, Middlesbrough

Blitz

The taste of smoke is trapped down my throat as I run to the shelter.
I could smell the sticky fumes drifting through the door.
I could see the planes speeding through the sky
While I was running to the shelter.
If I could touch the charred wood my hands would be black.
I wonder what my life brings me.

Hannah Cooke (10)
Nunthorpe Primary School, Middlesbrough

The Midnight Fox

The fox's tail is as long as an endless rope.
The sly, silent fox powerfully pounces on the small, white mouse.
Her fur is made up of gleaming stars.
She leads her children away from danger.
Quietly, quickly the fox hides from the loaded gun.
The fast, silent fox sprints across long, green grass.

Parice Imogen Lott (9)
Nunthorpe Primary School, Middlesbrough

The Midnight Fox

The mysterious black fox powerfully searches for her prey.
Black as a raven's shiny feathers she hunts.
Her eyes are gleaming gold flames.
Her teeth are like sharp daggers attacking.
Quickly pouncing to her enormous, brown den
And her soft, shiny tail is wiggling like jelly.

Taran Sidhu (9)
Nunthorpe Primary School, Middlesbrough

Blitz

All I could see was angry and fierce bombs dropping in
The background, carrying massive balls of ash with them.
The poisonous stench of burning ash clogs up my throat and lungs.
The destroyed wall felt rough with anger and scraped all my hands.
All I could smell was burning fires creating stenchy smoke.
My life is ruined.

Ethan Falcus (10)
Nunthorpe Primary School, Middlesbrough

The Midnight Fox

The fox is a sharp, silver knife cutting through the dim forest.
The sleek and silent fox spies on its prey.
She prances playfully through the gloomy, green forest.
Quietly, the fox darts into her dark den.
Her eyes are like two yellow glow sticks.
The powerful, sly fox roams quietly through the tall, green grass.

Sarah Jane April Roddam (9)
Nunthorpe Primary School, Middlesbrough

Howard Carter

Howard Carter found a mummy
In Egypt where it is always hot and sunny.
In a pyramid with lots of gold he found Tutankhamun,
He was very old.
Everybody was happy
To see Howard Carter's discovery.

Ebony Batty (7)
Nunthorpe Primary School, Middlesbrough

The Midnight Fox

The sleek and sly fox trots into the dense forest,
Graceful, sneakily the fox hunts her prey,
Powerfully she darts into the grave, gloomy wood,
The fox grins at me as she approaches her damp, dirty den,
Her fur is as inky as ravens' feathers,
She is the reflection of the moon dancing on sparkling water.

Ellie Grace Allport (9)
Nunthorpe Primary School, Middlesbrough

Blitz

Enemy planes drone menacingly from the dark ashy sky
Smoke fills my lungs as I walk down the dark smoky streets
I walk down gloomy streets tasting burnt tar
Climbing over fallen bricks as high as a mountain
Trying to escape my house
The sound of explosions and screaming deafened me.

Cameron Patrick Hutton (10)
Nunthorpe Primary School, Middlesbrough

Watching

The fox's tail is a coiled rope swaying high in the air.
She watches the mouse stealthily waiting to pounce.
She looks at me and smiles the mouse in her jaw.
Her teeth are sharp, shiny daggers.
Silently, swiftly she turns and walks into the forest.
Her fur is as dark as a starless sky.

Lewis Galloway (10)
Nunthorpe Primary School, Middlesbrough

The Midnight Fox

The fox's bushy fur is fluffy cotton wool,
Silent, sly, the fox hunts for her prey,
Sleepily, swiftly the fox pounces in the long, wavy grass,
She leaps like a flash of lightning in the sky,
She smoothly glides towards the hill.

Elycia Hutton Neil (9)
Nunthorpe Primary School, Middlesbrough

Around Egypt

E normous pyramids around the Valley of the Kings.
G ods are four - Isis, Osiris, Anubis and Horus.
Y ellow golden sand glittering all around.
P haraoh Tutankhamun was the most famous king.
T reasure on his mask was gold and blue.

Harry Forster (7)
Nunthorpe Primary School, Middlesbrough

The Midnight Fox

The midnight fox stares at her prey
Sneakily watching.
Her fur is as black as ink.
Eyes as sharp as daggers,
Fast and furious the fox loudly rips her prey.

Kieran Luke Stewart (9)
Nunthorpe Primary School, Middlesbrough

Chips

C risps are also made out of potatoes.
H eaps and heaps of chips for me please!
I love chip sandwiches with chips on the side.
P otatoes grow underground.
S pud is another name for potato.

Elise Hesk (7)
Nunthorpe Primary School, Middlesbrough

Blitz

Sharp splinters dig into my blood-stained knees.
I smell burning bodies, laying on the ground shouting for help.
Silence is shattered by bombs falling.
Bloodied, crumpled bodies lie on the rubbled ground.
The acrid taste of the greedy smoke soaks the fresh air.

Mazen Khabbass
Nunthorpe Primary School, Middlesbrough

Love

Love is colourful like a rainbow
When you're just sat watching it every afternoon.
But when you look at it, it's beautiful, it looks very pretty.
It smells like roses, just smelling very nice.
It sounds like someone you love, who loves you too very nicely.
It tastes like chocolate when you have just got it and eaten it.
When you are in love it feels loving in a way
Like someone is there with you every single day.
If you touch love it is very soft.
It reminds me of when I was just lying in my bed,
Just having a sip of milk in my baby bottle.
After that I would go to sleep
And my mum would look after and my dad.
So, my family loves me and that is all what matters.

Bethany Hall (9)
Rokeby Park Primary School, Hull

Happiness

Happiness is a delicate turquoise,
like the calming blue waves of the ocean.
Happiness is my family having fun at the jolly colourful fair.
Happiness smells lovely, like toasted marshmallows
being dipped in chocolate and covered in sprinkles.
Happiness sounds beautiful like birds tweeting in a tree.
Happiness tastes perfect, like my whole family
sitting down for a Sunday dinner.
Happiness feels like when I get a cheerful, loving hug from my family.
Happiness reminds me of love, like I love my family and friends.

Victoria Stamp (10)
Rokeby Park Primary School, Hull

Happiness

Happiness is yellow like the dazzling sun.
Happiness is smiley like big, red, rosy cheeks.
Happiness smells of juicy, big, fat apples.
Happiness sounds like the sound of wonderful laughter.
Happiness feels like you're in a big scented bush of beautiful flowers.
Happiness tastes like toasted, yummy marshmallows dipped
in chocolate.
Happiness reminds me of the sound of my mum laughing.
It feels like beautiful flowers on me.

Louise Langdon (8)
Rokeby Park Primary School, Hull

Love

Love is red like when you are embarrassed.
Love looks like a big red cheek.
Love tastes like a chocolate fountain.
Love feels like you going on dates.
Love reminds me of nice red roses.

Samiur Tarafdar (8)
Rokeby Park Primary School, Hull

Happiness

Happiness is yellow like the sun on a summer's day.
Happiness looks like a family enjoying themselves on a day out.
Happiness smells like melted, bubbling chocolate.
Happiness sounds like nature playing in a band.
Happiness tastes like marshmallows
Dipped in chocolate with strawberries.
Happiness feels like a velvety feather on my leg.
Happiness reminds me of my family.

Jordan Webb (9)
Rokeby Park Primary School, Hull

Love Is Wonderful

Love sounds like birds singing on a rainy day.
The colour of love is silver like the stars twinkling in the night sky.
Love looks like a wonderful rainbow on a bright sunny day.
Love smells like freshly cut grass on a summer's day.
Love tastes wonderful, like yummy toffee apples.
Love feels like warmth coming freshly from a burning fire.
Love reminds me of a chocolate fountain on a sparkling,
White winter's day.

Abbie Preston (8)
Rokeby Park Primary School, Hull

Love

Love is bright red flowers like a beautiful garden in full bloom.
Love smells like a chunk of melted chocolates in my mouth.
Love feels as joyful as a fluffy lamb in springtime.
Love tastes of marshmallows
Covered in the loveliest chocolate in the world.
Love reminds me of my kind family.
Love is my family.

Kayleigh Waller (9)
Rokeby Park Primary School, Hull

Peace

Peace is red like roses in bloom.
Peace is fresh like new grown daisies.
Peace is whispers of a gentle blowing wind.
Peace is the scent of fresh cut grass.
Peace is chocolate like sweet tea.
Peace is remarkable like good memories.
Peace is smooth like laminate floor.

Linden Price (9)
Rokeby Park Primary School, Hull

Anger Is Hot

Anger is red like scorching flames of fire.
Anger is frightening like a scary evil devil.
Anger smells like smoke coming from a bursting volcano.
Anger sounds like a beast getting ferociously mad.
Anger tastes like a curry with chilli peppers in.
Anger feels like an awful upsetting moment.
Anger reminds me of someone starting a fight with me.

Alexander Appleby (9)
Rokeby Park Primary School, Hull

Using Your Senses Of Love

The colour of love is white as the full moon.
Love looks like two people gazing into each other's eyes.
Love smells nice and sweet like Hull Fair.
Love sounds like people snogging.
Love tastes like delicious cherry drops.
Love feels good like lovely soft chocolate.
Love reminds me of Emily Scott.

Broady Aldred-Young (10)
Rokeby Park Primary School, Hull

Love

Love is all the colours of a beautiful rainbow.
Love looks like a big red heart.
Love smells of roses growing on a mountain top.
Love sounds like a sweet song.
Love tastes like my mummy's kisses.
Love is the feeling of happiness of everybody.
Love reminds me of my mum's hugs.

Breagh Boyle (8)
Rokeby Park Primary School, Hull

Love

Love reminds me of beautiful Cheryl Cole.
Love is like a rouge-red colour.
Love tastes of candyfloss.
Love sounds like two people kissing, mwah!
Love tastes like a chocolate apple.
Love feels like sunset.
Love feels marvellous.

Tom Jordan (9)
Rokeby Park Primary School, Hull

Love

Love is red like a heart full of kisses.
Love looks like a bouquet of roses and carnations.
Love sounds like people having fun at the fair.
Love tastes like sweet, sticky toffee apples and they are really good.
Love reminds me of the relaxing sunny beach.
Love is good and bad, it is good because people like each other,
it is bad because they fight.

Jodie Kerr (9)
Rokeby Park Primary School, Hull

Happiness

Happiness is yellow like the bright yellow sun.
Happiness smells like melting Galaxy chocolate
with squashy marshmallows.
Happiness sounds like a day at the fair.
Happiness feels like fluffy squashy teddy bears.
Happiness reminds me of going on holiday.
Happiness looks like big yellow smiley faces.

Bethany Scarr (9)
Rokeby Park Primary School, Hull

Fun

Fun is yellow like shimmering sun.
Fun looks like a pot of bright gold.
Fun smells like cotton candy whipped around the stick.
Fun sounds like a big, round, fat, sugary doughnut.
Fun feels like soft, fluffy pillows.
Fun reminds me of having fun with people and my friends.

Charlotte Mawston (9)
Rokeby Park Primary School, Hull

Love

Love is red like a family heart.
Love is warm as a new pair of slippers in front of the fire.
Love smells like lovely perfumed roses.
Love is the sound of children's laughter, loud and joyful.
Love smells like red beautiful roses swinging in the breeze.
Love reminds me of two people kissing.

Kara Bennett (9)
Rokeby Park Primary School, Hull

Fun

Fun is a pot of gold at the end of a rainbow.
Fun is like a big tower of silver.
Fun smells of brown milky chocolate.
Fun tastes like a tasty chocolatey chocolate fountain.
Fun feels like a big pot of freedom.
Fun reminds me of a magical park.

Enrico Perucho (9)
Rokeby Park Primary School, Hull

The Taste Of Fear Filled The Air

Oozing thick mud plasters my creased grey trousers,
As I plod on towards the battlefield.
Goosebumps prickle up,
Fear creeps into my body.

Tanks roll towards us,
Ready to start a ferocious battle.
Soldiers fall to the ground,
Dying from exhaustion.
Miles of armed forces,
Heading towards us.

Bullets rapidly firing at us,
Flying past my aching head.
Screams as people gradually fall to the ground.
Exploding bombs, heard in any direction.

Bloodstained top,
Sticking to my sweaty back.
Hard metal gun
Clasped in my clammy hand.
Feel the pain of the dying men.

As I lick my dry lips,
The taste of blood fills my mouth,
The taste of fear filled the air.

Eve Armstrong (10)
St John the Evangelist RC School, Billingham

The Experience Of A Fighting Man

All the possible sweat pouring down your clammy shivering skin.
Fear grabbed your blood covered body,
As you take one step at a time into battle.
Horrifying wounds on allies,
Once they have been hit
By silver iron bullets at full force.

Once again, you could hear
The bullets whizzing through the air,
Trying to strike their enemies,
Cause huge wreckage on the opponent,
Whilst feeling a bloodstained uniform
On an injured soldier.

His gun shivering in his sweat covered hands
As he prepares to encounter enemies.
Mud from the swamp,
Slowly crawling up his aching leg.
Terrifying bombs being fired,
Like lightning out the black jet skies.
Poisonous gas filled the whole perimeter,
Air from a terrifying gas attack.

God please save my family,
And my best friend.
Hopefully this war will eventually end.

Ryan Blackett (10)
St John the Evangelist RC School, Billingham

Lord Please!

Terror creeping around,
Prayers to live are heard.
Orders are given to fight.
His heavy parachute pulling on his back,
Dark red lights turn to bright green.
Lord, please help him!

White parachutes falling by the dozen;
Hot sparks as the Germans shoot.
Gooey sweat dripping to Earth!
Screams are heard as soldiers die.
Lord, please help him!

Landing on lush green grass,
Soldiers charge at the Germans,
Taking cover behind ancient walls.
Metal monsters crashing down trees.
Lord, please . . .

Medics putting him on a wagon,
Pulling him home to rest.
'Gas, gas, quick boys, let's leave him.'
His eyes are white, his heart stopped beating.
Lord, please receive him.

Jason Diggle (10)
St John the Evangelist RC School, Billingham

The Memories Of A Fighting Soldier

Touching the gun with his bare hands.
Searching for men in the forbidden lands.
Friends falling like children learning to walk,
In this land there is no time to talk.

Bullets zooming past his head.
Be careful my young regiment said.
Thinking of his wife, hoping she is not dead.
Going into battle with a bloodstained head.

Bombs dropping overhead.
People receiving telegraphs saying loved ones are dead.
Stumbling to walk, he knows he must keep going.
Another man down, he could be next.
Soldiers' muscles are tight and legs are sore.

Vera Lynn singing on the radio very softly.
Guns shouting and people screaming.
He is lucky to be alive.
He doesn't want his life to end,
With everything to lose,
His wife, his family and friends.

News strikes out, the war is over but his journey is far from o . . .

Rhiannon Clayton (11)
St John the Evangelist RC School, Billingham

The Magic Box

(Based on 'Magic Box' by Kit Wright)

I will put in my box . . .
The laugh of a child as she joyfully peers at her newborn sister
The first smile of parents when their daughter discovers snow
The wish to be a successful writer.

I will put in my box . . .
The old raggy frill of an extremely special blanket
snuggled up at home
The memory of my first Christmas - a giant teddy for me
waiting under a tall tree glittering silently
The tear of sadness when my great grandma silently died
a few days after her birthday.

I will put in my box . . .
Happy families playing with each other
A spooky sleepover where noises could be heard
The grin from my favourite forever friend, Ellie.

My box is fashioned with happiness, friendship and joy
The corners are full of secrets
The hinges are gold.

Katie Mowbray (8)
St John the Evangelist RC School, Billingham

Fire Breathing Bombs That Fell

Suddenly ricocheting bullets started travelling at great speed.
Fear grabbed his sweat-covered skin,
Muscles tightened under bloodstained clothes.
Petrified people screaming their hearts out.
A dark ominous monster approached the grey gloomy sky.
Fire breathing bombs that fell,
More than fifty died.

Acid burning in his dry mouth,
Gas filled up in his lungs,
More and more sweat
Dripping down on the soldier's crippled, twisted back,
At every jolt blood came gargling
From his corrupted throat.

Terrified children and adults shaking side to side,
Mud crawling up the soldier's leather boots.
Like lightning, a terrifying bomb went off,
Soldiers started talking,
Then suddenly stopped!
Smoke and gas filled the jet-black sky.

Megan Sobotowska (10)
St John the Evangelist RC School, Billingham

Things You'd Find
In A Bombed Out House

(Based on 'Ten Things Found In A Wizard's Pocket' by Ian McMillan)

Teddy bears' stuffing scattered across the bloodstained carpet.
A half-open telegram resting on the fire-covered arm rest.
Air raid wardens scanning the rubble for survivors.
An elderly man's hand reaching out for help.
A young boy lying dead upon the carpet.
Vera Lynn's voice becoming fainter as the bombing becomes
stronger.

Amy Harris (10)
St John the Evangelist RC School, Billingham

Soldier's Bravery

Thick oozing mud travels up a soldier's bloodstained trousers.
He plods through the swamp.
Bombshells land on the cratered ground.
Pulling the trigger on the gun,
To shoot the enemy as the guns make a shockingly loud sound.
Big black holes form in his heart,
Knowing that his wife is dead.

He is relieved that his children
Are safely evacuated to Canada.
Also scared in case they never return.
Bullets speeding towards him.
Luftwaffe aircraft flying overhead.

Why couldn't he be safe at home instead?
Where in Canada are his children?
One Doodlebug landed before him.
He could have been dead like his wife!
He dodged the explosion,
Then saved his friend's life.

Jodie Hall (10)
St John the Evangelist RC School, Billingham

A Man Of War!

Tank shells vibrating the hollow ground as they violently hit.
Heartbroken as my best friend gets shot by the enemy.
More bombs drop one by one as they explode onto the soggy earth.
Reinforcements to strengthen the falling army to win the battle.
Clutching my deadly gun, aiming, firing.
Hanging on for dear life, always thinking about my gorgeous wife.
Dangerous monsters flying here and there but always finding its prey.
German soldiers starting to retreat, 'Come on lads,' said my captain,
'let's be on our way.'
Toxic gas comes again, faster and faster,
Can I get my gas mask on in . . .

Kai Adams (10)
St John the Evangelist RC School, Billingham

The Brave Soldier

Screams of pain as more and more soldiers fall like apples
from an old oak tree.
Whizzing as bombs violently smack the cracked ground.
Heart torn into pieces as he reads the letter he had hoped
never to receive (his family are dead).
Scared and now alone, he has just lost his best friend -
Who will stay by his side now?
Soldiers' life and memories erased as deadly Doodlebugs
randomly fall.
Rocket glaring down on soldiers, while they rush
to sludge-filled shelters.
Dry sand rubbed against his legs, as he struggles
to make it through the battlefield.
Bloodstained sweat trickling down an opened wound on his leg.
Foul burning taste trickling the sores on his taste buds.
Gas tightly wrapped his lungs as he rushed to his gas mask
- too slow!

Sophie Mulloy (10)
St John the Evangelist RC School, Billingham

The Experience Of A Battle

Muscles tensing as the heart pounds with terror.
Sweat covered skin crawling with incredible fear.
Men charging across the battlefield,
Stumbling one after another.
Dark monsters howling in the sky overhead.

Generals giving orders to blood-shot soldiers,
Guns firing, mortars exploding, men dying.
Toxic smoke blowing in the gentle winds.
Poisonous gas spreading across the battlefield.

German goods stolen from an abandoned camp,
Dead soldiers' body parts,
Touch shaking legs.

Elliot Wing (10)
St John the Evangelist RC School, Billingham

The Soldier

Thick, brown, squelchy mud
Oozed out onto his creased leather boots,
Bloodstained trousers.
Sweat trickled down his camouflaged face,
Memories of friends,
Family burrowed in his head.

Bullets whizzing through the air,
Bombs landing
Just a few feet away.
Thick black smoke rises
Through the gas-filled air.
Every person with a gas mask.

Someone was unlucky,
He did not raise his mask in time.
More pain to come,
There is no cure, he is already dead.

Brittany Munson (10)
St John the Evangelist RC School, Billingham

The Magic Box

(Based on 'Magic Box' by Kit Wright)

I will put in my box . . .
the sound of noisy fireworks crashing loudly among the huge hills,
the smells of sizzling sausages popping in the frying pan,
my wish to become a graceful ballerina.

I will put in my box . . .
a disgusting smell of burnt toast when a toaster has blown up,
the horrifying sound of grinding teeth when my sister is bored,
a laugh of joy when I rub my head on my sister's tummy.

My box is fashioned with swans' graceful, fluffy feathers.
In the corner there are beautiful red rubies.
Its hinges are made out of golden crowns.

Ellie Mulligan (8)
St John the Evangelist RC School, Billingham

A Soldier Of War

Tank shells vibrating the ground
As they violently hit.
Heart pounding with the fear of never coming back.
Muscles tightening every second,
Feet sinking into the sloppy mud.

Bullets whizzing past my eyes,
Friends falling to the ground,
As they lose their lives.
Everywhere I look,
Death is there.

Dangerous things everywhere I turn,
Danger around every corner,
Sound of fear in everyone
I taste the gas on my lungs,
O God, here he comes.

Amber Lavender (11)
St John the Evangelist RC School, Billingham

During The Blitz You May Discover

(Based on 'Ten Things Found In A Wizard's Pocket' by Ian McMillan)

Ashes blowing cautiously in the wind.
Nervous people begging anxiously for life.
While the smell of smoke grows larger and larger,
Choking the throats of innocent people.
Someone sobbing loudly trying to find a sister.
Chess pieces scattered everywhere as if they were dropped
suddenly.
Demolished dens from long ago.
Bring back flashbacks from a long time ago.
75 long days in London.
The all-clear wailing loudly.
And that's what you would discover during the Blitz.

Bethany Hunton (9)
St John the Evangelist RC School, Billingham

Fighting In The War

Thick mud climbing up my wounded leg,
Ricocheted bullets fly towards me.
They hit ancient walls.
Screams of terror in all directions,
My muscles tighten anxiously.

Sweat trickles down my forehead,
Shattered gas mask on dry land,
Bullets trespassing into bodies,
Hearts torn into pieces,
Families are gone,
Toxic smoke rising in the distance.

Fear and despair gripping hearts,
Guns of the Axis due to die,
What right Is it to due for your country?
Is the battlefield victory?

Emily Hyndman (10)
St John the Evangelist RC School, Billingham

In A Bombed Out House

(Based on 'Ten Things Found In A Wizard's Pocket' by Ian McMillan)

In a bombed out house you would find:
Shattered glass,
An old man shivering with a photograph of a family member clutched
tightly in his hand,
A little boy screaming for his mother,
The ARP searching frantically for injured people,
A worried father leaning on the bloodstained walls looking for his
beloved children,
Stuffing of a loved teddy bear scattered across the floor,
Cackling sounds from the radio that can be heard from a distance,
That is what you would find in a bombed out house!

Liam Monaghan (9)
St John the Evangelist RC School, Billingham

101

I'll Be The Next One Dead!

(World War II, 1939-1945)

Clinging to the trigger of a freezing gun,
Things were happening that were so not fun.

We searched and searched until the moon came out,
We looked in the waters full of trout.

Until days later they found a trace,
Of a poor young man with a bloodstained face.

With all the blood he had shed,
He shall lie on a hand-made death bed.

I fear that I'll be the next in a box,
Put in the ground and covered with rocks.

After all it was my father,
I love him lots . . .

Jamie Allison (11)
St John the Evangelist RC School, Billingham

The Experience Of A Man In Battle

Thick mud climbed up my wounded leg.
Sweat slid down my jet-black forehead.
Screams of terror came from every direction.

Muscles tightened as fear and despair gripped my heart.
Ricocheting bullets travelled across the battleground
at a great speed.
Men fell as powerful bullets invaded them.

Dangerous illuminated monsters roared above my head.
Loud commands from chiefs screaming
for the sake of their country.
I know that soon I will . . .

Olivia Smith (10)
St John the Evangelist RC School, Billingham

The Magic Box

(Based on 'Magic Box' by Kit Wright)

I will put in my box . . .
A fearsome dragon that burns down the city which blows out fireballs
whilst terrorising the city,
The funniest memory that made me laugh my socks off,
My wish is to become a really fancy footballer
that scores 1000 goals.

I will put in my box . . .
A frightful memory of when I heard a huge bang,
It made me jump out of my skin,
The spooky sight of my sister when she gives me an evil look.

My box is fashioned with a graceful white feather,
With colourful flower petals and shiny red rubies.
Its hinges are the horns of a fairy devil.

Joseph Armstrong (8)
St John the Evangelist RC School, Billingham

The Terrors Of The Front

Thick mud climbing up creased leather boots.
Heartbeat rate accelerating,
Tension growing.
Friends dying after cruel Nazi shots.
Bombs crashing near a tank that was towing.

Screams of dying men filled the air.
Bloodstained uniforms turned hands red with pouring blood.
Soldiers dying as their clothes tear.
Men trying to stop war if they only could.

Poisoning tastes of deadly gas in his lungs.
Enemies ready to unleash a deadly attack.
Gas settling on soldiers' tongues.
Blood mixing with the sweat
And dripping down his crippled back.

Oliver Cox (10)
St John the Evangelist RC School, Billingham

The Blitz

(Based on 'Ten Things Found In A Wizard's Pocket' by Ian McMillan)

During the Blitz you may discover;
Fearsome fires putting buildings out of existence,
Lightning striking heavily on high towers,
Dogs searching for owners,
Adults searching, children lost,
Wires weaving wildly through walls,
Burning flames spreading everywhere,
Smoke spreading more every minute,
And that's what you may discover during the Blitz.

Lauren Parsons (9)
St John the Evangelist RC School, Billingham

The Autumn Sights

I watch as the crunchy, cracked leaves
scatter from the old parent, the tree
and are whisked away
by the chilled autumn wind.

I see the birds meeting others
on our cold, slippery rooftops
ready to fly away
to another warmer place.

Also, the children searching the old tree for conkers
and the happiness on some faces is lovely
But the young boy, struggling to find any
runs to his father, crying and wailing.

The smoke from the bonfire
is being blown away by the howling winds
to the old man's house
deep in the countryside.

Myles Kirk (11)
St Robert's RC Primary School, Harrogate

Autumn's Beauty

The world is glowing!
It is full of colour,
For autumn is here,
Summer has gone.

Dogs and children play in the leaves,
Up comes a dog with muddy paws,
Even the countryside has changed,
With streaks of purple across the moors.

In the orchard, green apples hang,
Flushed bright pink by a shining sun.
They leave a wonderful fruity tang,
Which attracts the last of the butterflies in swirling masses.

Mist hangs on the hillside,
Pierced only by the sharp beaks of birds,
Flying south with a swirl and a glide,
Over the farmers, dogs and herds.

The sun dips low,
And as it disappears,
Gives off a warming glow,
The red tinted glow of autumn's glory.

There's a change in the people too,
As they note autumn's arrival.
Gloves, scarves and hats stick to them like glue,
That won't come off until spring comes again.

Autumn notes the season for fires,
But also for wonderful beauty,
A beauty like in no other season.
Autumn has come again!

Fionnuala Murphy (10)
St Robert's RC Primary School, Harrogate

Autumn's Here Again

Autumn's here again
Skies turning a wintry grey
Children kicking leaves higher and higher
Smoke floating through the air from the fires.

Autumn's here again
Winds whistle in the darkness
Soon it will be Christmas
Leaves turning gold, scarlet, rose and crimson.

Autumn's here again
Flowers vanish from our eyes
People preparing for the snow
Whether it will come I don't know.

Autumn's here again.

Elena Brown (10)
St Robert's RC Primary School, Harrogate

Autumn Days

Autumn days have come so quick
Leaves glowing full of colour
Lying in the street
Children kicking topaz leaves
Looking for their first conker
Autumn days have come so quick
Winds blowing leaves around and around
As if stuck in a whirlpool
All you can see is a sea of crimson
Autumn days have come so quick
Trees swaying in the autumn winds
Smoke flying high with the clouds
Autumn days are here.

Patrick Tunstall (10)
St Robert's RC Primary School, Harrogate

The Warmth Of Autumn

Trees sway slowly to retain their dignity
as proud leaves dance around them.
Wind whistles sadly through the leaf-littered floor.
Skies, pinks, golden and a hint of blue, fading into the darkness.
Leaves crimson, damp and muddy, kick them up in the air.
Birds swoop from half-naked branches
to join the flock of friends flying south.
Smoke from fires in backyards and chimneys
leaves glowing reminders in the air the next morning.
Children with looks of pure delight scavenge for chestnuts
among the piles of rusty leaves.
See faces light up as they pocket one,
Ready to roast on the fire tonight.

Georgina Sheerin (11)
St Robert's RC Primary School, Harrogate

Autumn Is Here

Trees whistle with the wind,
Dark crimson leaves cascade through the peaceful sapphire sky,
Children hunt for hidden conkers beneath the piles of leaves,
Trees stand strong and tall, although naked and bare,
Birds soar through the sky, meet and depart for warmer lands,
Smoke whirls high above,
Fires are as red as a ruby,
A scarlet texture in the night,
Autumn is here.

Sarah Cunningham (10)
St Robert's RC Primary School, Harrogate

Witches' Brew

Down in the dungeon,
Dark and damp,
As cold as winter's night,
No one knows she's there,
Hunched and crooked she stoops,
With a walking stick and hissing cat,
She bends over her bubbling brew.

Slimy skin of snake,
Juicy red eyeballs ready to pop,
Tail of lizard electric blue stripes and thunder spots,
Legs of frogs and wings of bats,
Slimy skin of shark,
Black toenails of werewolf.

Round and round the cauldron,
Round and round it goes,
Stirring the poisonous poison,
Nobody knows . . .

Ami Moore, Sadie Rose Palmer, Alex Sexton
& Samuel Smith (9)
Sutton Park Primary School, Hull

The Time Of Autumn

Hedgehogs hibernating under a pile of crunchy leaves,
Lying sleepily,
Rats scurrying, sniffing for food,
Whistling leaves on the dying trees - with a squirrel making its home,
Bears hibernating, cosy in their cave,
Bats swooping in the air,
Frogs jumping from lilypad to lilypad,
Moles digging molehills,
The dying time for salmon is here,
Butterflies' eggs being laid,
Autumn time has come.

Jessica Merryn Smith & Jessica Bradford (9)
Sutton Park Primary School, Hull

Horrific Hallowe'en!

Shocking spiders
Scaring kids,
Black horrid legs
Scurrying everywhere.

Vicious vampires
Sucking people's blood,
Petrified people screaming.

Wicked witches
On their brooms,
In the moonlit sky,
Putting spells on people as they fly.

Dreadful devils
Looking suspicious,
In the night,
Blood everywhere.

Macy Wiles (10) & Ellie Spence (9)
Sutton Park Primary School, Hull

Weather

Some days are sunny,
Some days are damp,
Some days are funny,
Some days are perfect for camp.

Some days are nice,
Some days are cold,
Some days are perfect for mice,
But the fruit turns to mould,
When it's cold.

Nathan Higgins & Callum Lane (9)
Sutton Park Primary School, Hull

Christmas

Christmas is a happy time when Santa comes
And shocks a few mums,
When half their carrots and beer
Suddenly disappear!

Dasher, Dancer, Rudolph and the rest,
Mary, Joseph, Jesus Christ,
Christmas dinner, that's the best,
Red, gold, silver too,
Hang your baubles up, now you!

Santa, snowmen, snow on the grass,
Snow everywhere, come on lass!
Snowball fighting,
Candle lighting,
Jumping on the lawn,
What crisps do you like, was it prawn?

Paris Pidd (9)
Sutton Park Primary School, Hull

Swaps

I will give you:

A slimy slug
A small dog
A yellow mug
A big ship
A tiny jug
A red door
A garden bug
A skull head
And a lovely hug

For your DVD
What do you say?
No!

James Scottow (10)
Sutton Park Primary School, Hull

110

Swaps

I'll give you:

A pussycat
A colourful book
A tiny rat
A swirly rock
A yellow hat
A large canoe
A creepy bat
A scary skeleton
And a fluffy mat

For your PSP
What do you say?
No!

James Short (11)
Sutton Park Primary School, Hull

Fishes

Orange, spotty, bubbly, slimy, disgusting fish,
Orange, swishy, slithery, stinky, disgusting fish,
Orange, slodgy, loud, bumpy, mysterious, disgusting fish,
Orange, glittery, peaceful, smooth, smelly, disgusting fish,
Colourful, colourful, colourful, fishy, fishy, fishy . . .

Little orange fishes swimming in the gleaming water,
Little orange fishes eating their food,
Little orange fishes dancing in the water,
Colourful, colourful, colourful, fishy, fishy, fishy . . .

Mikyla Victoria Dillon & Mogan Bellamy (9)
Sutton Park Primary School, Hull

Hallowe'en

H owling wolves in the midnight darkness,
A ncient zombies under your bed,
L ight the street up with your lanterns,
L oneliness in the dark,
O range pumpkins with big bright faces,
W icked witches in the sky,
E xtraordinary skeletons made of bones,
E xciting mummies in the street,
N ever-ending fear.

Ashley Ferguson (10) & Jarrod Scott (9)
Sutton Park Primary School, Hull

Untitled

The moon is white
It is so bright
That's why it shines at night
It is made out of cheese
Like yellow bees
It's light that's right
But at night it's so bright
It is as round as an apple.

Kelvyn MacLeod (10)
Sutton Park Primary School, Hull

Hallowe'en

Dawn in the darkness
Rattling his bones
It's the skeleton that moans and groans.

Big fat pumpkins lighting up the street
Loads of mummies losing their feet
For the vampire that's a treat.

Tom Cracknell (9), Harvey Marritt (10) & Jack Love
Sutton Park Primary School, Hull

112

Hallowe'en

Hallowe'en is my favourite night
We watch people have a fight
Little people knocking on the door
Getting sweets as they walk
Giving people a little fright
Watch the scary ghost fly up in the dark night.

Chloe Jade Wilson & Megan Williams (10)
Sutton Park Primary School, Hull

Autumn Fox

On an autumn day,
the grass was green,
some leaves were on the trees,
some were not.

The dark fox
scavenged mysteriously
for food.

His crown made of golden leaves
was swiftly falling
in the wind.

The steaming hot sun
was in the background,
all of the trees were empty,
no leaves on them.

Just the branches
the leaves were softly floating
down the river.

Jodie Simpson (9)
Wavell Junior School, Catterick Garrison

The Magnificent Robins

Robins are here
Robins are there
Robins, robins
They are everywhere.

Robins are fast
Robins can sing
Robins, robins
What's the matter with these things.

Robins are smart
Robins can think
Robins, robins
What smart things.

Robins are cute
Robins are sweet
Robins, robins
What a treat.

Craig Riley (9)
Wavell Junior School, Catterick Garrison

I Really Miss My Dad,

It makes me really mad.
Every time he goes away,
All I do is pray and pray.

I miss the touch of his hand,
He has the softest skin in the land.
Why does he have to fight?
I dream about him every night.

I sometimes start to cry,
I don't have the faintest idea why.
All I know is I miss my dad,
I miss my dad like mad.

Dionne Jones (10)
Wavell Junior School, Catterick Garrison

A Child's Wish

Bombs, bombs everywhere
Bombs, bombs such a scare
War is here, war is there, war is nearly everywhere.

War is bad, war is wrong
Soldiers have been fighting far too long!
Please stop, have a break
Stop this war for goodness sake!

People are hurt, people are dying,
Families at home are always crying,
Women and children and the neighbours next door
Don't want this fight anymore!

Our rivers are red
because of our dead
let the fighting cease,
may our world live in peace.

Kora Dollimore (10)
Wavell Junior School, Catterick Garrison

The Dinosaur

People dancing in a ballroom,
Calm as a bird twittering.
Flittering in a tall calm tree,
People dancing and dancing,
Suddenly the music gets faster,
Like a crocodile coming with an enormous roaring mouth,
Twirling dinosaur
Coming top speed,
It slows like a hippo
Walking slowly and fiercely
Like a shark coming
To kill somebody,
It slowly ends.

Nathan Hill-Tuft (0)
Wavell Junior School, Catterick Garrison

Come Back Tomorrow

How I yearn for his gentle smile,
But I have to endure all the while;
Every time I walk out the door,
I think of you more and more.

My whole body is hollow
Sleepless nights, they always follow;
This war is piercing my heart
Hoping my love will come back tomorrow.

You are my whole life,
And you are my joy,
Then why should it all go and destroy?

I love you more than I can say
And will always do, day by day.

Garima Rai (11)
Wavell Junior School, Catterick Garrison

Hallowe'en's Here

Hallowe'en's here
Ghosts are near
Can't you hear the signs of rustling trees.
Spooky night in the light,
Faces you may not know,
Kidnappers in the glow . . .
Trick or treating
Candy face flying in the air,
Bats are hairy
But witches are scary
Skeletons rattling everywhere
Darkness and despair
Witches' brooms and scary rooms
Ghosts of the past lying in their tombs.

Orianna Langley (8)
Wavell Junior School, Catterick Garrison

The Autumn Salamander

Autumn salamander, prince of the harvest,
I have seen you glowing in the delicate sun,
With your amethyst body
Glinting in the sun.
Your eyes shine like 1,000 rubies
And your tail stretches on for 10,000 miles.
On your side we watch the sunrise.
Your toes sparkle with jewels.
Your horns sway in the breeze.
You sit upon your branch and watch the bright sun rise.
Autumn salamander you are here at last.
You move delicately in the sun.
Your scarlet scales glint as you move into the amber sun.

Craig Ottaway (9)
Wavell Junior School, Catterick Garrison

Autumn Snake

Autumn snake is here
King I have seen the sunset
I hear you rustling in the wind
You fall all over me when it is windy
I see your golden belly on the horizon
And hear you whistle in the air
I hear you crashing in the darkness
We feel you spitting on us
The cool air breathing on me
I feel you slap me with your strong headstone
Your beautiful ruby eyes and your wonderful amethyst nose
I thank you for all your great fruit
Autumn snake we are proud of you, thank you.

Jack Harrold (9)
Wavell Junior School, Catterick Garrison

I Really Miss My Dad

I really miss my dad,
Everyone thinks I'm mad,
I'm lonesome for my dad,
I feel so bad.

I hope my dad doesn't get into fright,
I wish he'd come back from that other land,
I pray for him every night,
Nor when he's stuck I wish he could get a helping hand.

Mom cries for her sweetheart,
I feel so shy,
If something happened to him,
I would curl and die.

Taylor Wright (11)
Wavell Junior School, Catterick Garrison

The Magical Unicorn

Unicorn, unicorn, grant me a wish,
Make me fly to the sky-high sun,
With your jewelled eyes
And your sparkling fur and the sun by your side.

Unicorn, unicorn, don't go away,
I need your autumn magic,
As you walk by the trees
All the leaves fall by your side.

Please don't go when I go to sleep
You will be in my heart forever
Autumn unicorn.

Jade Colligan (10)
Wavell Junior School, Catterick Garrison

The Old House

The old house stands at the top of the hill
blackened, silent and still.

They say on dark nights you can hear
the ghost's laughter, a cry of fear.

That you can see beside the wall
a shadowy figure gaunt and tall,
clutching a bundle wrapped in a cloak.

That you can see the swirling smoke
and hear the crackling of the fire
and watch flames leap higher and higher.

Brittany Dennison (10)
Wavell Junior School, Catterick Garrison

Autumn Snake

Autumn snake is here
The king of harvest
I have seen your sunny crown
With your golden mane blowing in the breezy air
Your sun crown has your ruby leaves all around
As your rainbow belly stretches across the horizon
You slither across the colourful leaves
Your amber eyes glowing
Leaves falling all around you
Your spiked leaves on the tip of your tail
Your amethyst nose sniffing the things around you.

Lewis Keane (9)
Wavell Junior School, Catterick Garrison

Hallowe'en

Red leaves on the tree falling down on the ground.
Flashing up in the dark, dark sky.
Zooming, up high, high, high.
Leaves fling around the place,
Everyone screaming in the dark, dark moonlight.
In the dark sky up, up high
Ghosts flying around the creepy weary place.
When you knock on the door you get a creepy fright.
Bats next to your house fluttering by your side.
Green flies, gulls' beaks, gizzard of gun,
Mix them well Mrs Stoge we want a lovely stick treat.

Emma Lawrie (8)
Wavell Junior School, Catterick Garrison

World War II

My father's in hospital,
I hope he's safe and sound,

I hope he's going to come home,
He got hit to the ground.

Now he's home,
We're all glad,

We're one big family,
And it will stay like this
For as long as we live.

Charlie Skelton (10)
Wavell Junior School, Catterick Garrison

The Queen

The Queen walked down the hill to the castle.
The Queen walked down the hill with a smile on her face
To her castle.
Things weren't the same.
There was a man at the castle.
The Queen let him in.
She fell in love with him.
He fell in love with her.
They married at once
And they were King and Queen.

Georgia Hill-Tuft (8)
Wavell Junior School, Catterick Garrison

Hallowe'en

Big breeze from the trees
Little children eating beans
Fireworks going gleam to gleam
People working in the beams.
Stars glisten in the air
Trees standing tall and bare.
People talking nice and tall
Roar, roar! Knock on the door.
Trick or treaters at the door
Give me a sweet or something more.

Aaron Skelton (8)
Wavell Junior School, Catterick Garrison

Autumn

Whizzing, sizzling
Loud booms in the air
Colours pop above your house
And garden with a big *boom!*

Niall Stott (8)
Wavell Junior School, Catterick Garrison

The Autumn Peacock

On the autumn day
The harvest stays today, the sun is yellow
The flowers are growing and the animals are dancing
There is an autumn peacock growing fruits and trees
She opens her feathers which glow like the sun
Ruby jewelled and orange beak
With a crown golden leaf
She opens her beak and sings
Thank you autumn peacock
For the fruits and flowers.

Shusil Malla (9)
Wavell Junior School, Catterick Garrison

The Cupboard

The trumpet went quiet
The treasure box went gold
Then boom! It was gone to dust!
It went chatter, whirring, mad, like a mission
It stopped
The blue ceiling was cracking
It cracked on the teacher of evil
She was lying there
In the cupboard of doom
She was dead!

Chandler Galliers-Allison (8)
Wavell Junior School, Catterick Garrison

Tree

One tiny seed can turn into a tree
Grow it in your garden and wait and see!
Apple trees, orange trees and pear trees too!
Growing fruit for me and you!

Caitlin Jones (7)
Wavell Junior School, Catterick Garrison

Walking Through The Park

Walking through the park what do I see?
A big fat oak tree with a key.

Walking through the park what do I see?
An old man making a little fee.

A caterpillar, oh what a surprise
And an alien butterfly with four big eyes.

Walking through the park what a wonderful place
And you do it at your own pace.

Regan Senior (10)
Wavell Junior School, Catterick Garrison

I Want To Go Home

I want to go home
I want to go home
I don't want to be here anymore
I am mad, bad, dad,
I am freaked out like dads mostly always are.

I was so scared,
Cannons roaring like a thousand lions.

I must not fear, I don't want to stay here.

Connor Dagnall (10)
Wavell Junior School, Catterick Garrison

The Autumn Peacock

On the autumn days
We see the peacock
You see her wings blowing in the wind
You can hear her amber feet swishing in the leaves
And her jewelled feathers in the darkness
She glows up in the night.

Mikey Cottingham (9)
Wavell Junior School, Catterick Garrison

Autumn Fox

The fox was rustling
Through the fiery glowing leaves
The sky was a beautiful blue colour
With white puffing clouds
The autumn fox's eyes were a mysterious golden brown

The autumn fox's tail was a bushy furry amber colour
Then the autumn fox
Quickly drifted through the misty forest.

Brooke Jones (9)
Wavell Junior School, Catterick Garrison

I'm An Evacuee

I am an evacuee,
From out at sea,
I'm an evacuee,
Please help me.

I'm an evacuee,
From a war zone,
I'm an evacuee,
I want a peaceful home.

Laura May McDermott (11)
Wavell Junior School, Catterick Garrison

I Want My Dad To Come Back

I miss the warmth of his hands,
The kisses when we said goodnight,
It was the highlight of my day,
He reminds me of the past delight.

Our hearts are aching because of Dad,
We try to forget about the sorrow,
We try to forget there might not be a tomorrow.

Yashika Bahik (11)
Wavell Junior School, Catterick Garrison

Monday's Child

Monday's child is always healthy,
Tuesday's child is very wealthy,
Wednesday's children is full of gladness,
Thursday's child is full of sadness,
Friday's child is very caring,
Saturday's child is always daring,
But the child who is born on a Sunday
Has a kind and clever mind.

Charlotte Brown (7)
Wavell Junior School, Catterick Garrison

The Day I Got Sent To War

I got sent to war the other day
The enemy try to shoot me like I'm a tiger's prey
Every day soldiers die
Planes get blown up sky high
We stuff all our things in our sacks
Watching people die sends a shiver down our backs
I see bodies with sticking-out bones
All I want to do is go home.

Brok Hollingworth (10)
Wavell Junior School, Catterick Garrison

The Softly Swaying River

A rabbit running across a grassy field
Two people dancing to a swift piece of music
Fish quickly swimming down a softly swaying river
A little girl running quickly but elegantly to see the Queen
The bird quickly flew down past a stream
At a concert crowds of people were staring at the clouds
People were playing the flute
When the owls were starting to hoot.

Eleanor Kilvington (8)
Wavell Junior School, Catterick Garrison

The Dancing Deer Of Autumn

Amber eyes dancing through the golden leaves,
Autumn, autumn, autumn is here!
Prancing and dancing through the autumn wood
Autumn, autumn, autumn is here!
Deer are delicate like little golden leaves,
Autumn, autumn, autumn is here!
Ruby red shining fur, glittering jewelled hooves,
Autumn, autumn, autumn is here!

Kasey Kenyon & Megan Burke (9)
Wavell Junior School, Catterick Garrison

The Autumn Fox

The orange fur of a scarlet fox
is just like orange leaves in autumn
The fearful fox is soft like leaves
and the beautiful fur is just like a fiery sun
The tail swishes like leaves when the wind comes
The fox walks like a delicate leaf
that the wind has blown away
and touches the ground lightly.

Dicchya Pun (9)
Wavell Junior School, Catterick Garrison

The Hedgehog Of Autumn

The hedgehog of autumn moves softly
Through the gentle breeze of the autumn,
Its violet robe smoothly flies across the horizon
And its pattering feet echo through the wood.
Its jewelled eyes shine on the Earth
And its golden fur is as soft as moss.
The spikes are as sharp as a rose thorn,
The colour of the autumn leaves.

Dafydd Lewis (10)
Wavell Junior School, Catterick Garrison

The Autumn Peacock

I saw this thing today, it looked like a peacock.
It was rustling in the leaves, it was a remarkable sight,
With its golden beak squawking at me.
All the leaves fell down before it.
All the trees swung before its beautiful amber feathers.
Its amethyst body stands out before you,
Standing there with its fragile legs,
It's spectacular.

Laura McGregor (9)
Wavell Junior School, Catterick Garrison

Untitled

Monday's child is always healthy,
Tuesday's child is always wealthy,
Wednesday's child is always caring,
Thursday's child is very daring,
Friday's child is always kind,
Saturday's child has a great mind,
But the child born on a Sunday
Always gets his own way!

Mia Canavan (7)
Wavell Junior School, Catterick Garrison

Untitled

Monday's child is always healthy,
Tuesday's child is nice and wealthy,
Wednesday's child is funny and bubbly,
Thursday's child is untidy and stubbly,
Friday's child is always in need,
Saturday's child is handsome indeed,
But the child who is born on Sunday
Is caring and daring.

Ben Davies (7)
Wavell Junior School, Catterick Garrison

I Want To Come Home

I want to come home
I want to come home
It's too scary here
I don't know anyone
I'm too full of fear
I miss you Mum
I miss your hugs and kisses
I just want to be home again.

Lauren Duffy (10)
Wavell Junior School, Catterick Garrison

Untitled

Monday's child is always healthy,
Tuesday's child is always wealthy,
Wednesday's child has many brothers,
Thursday's child is helpful to others,
Friday's child is very scary,
Saturday's child is really hairy,
But the child who is born on Sunday
Plays and is full of joy.

Reece Mahoney (7)
Wavell Junior School, Catterick Garrison

Tears Of War

I missed you every night,
He used to tuck me into bed,
Every night I pray to God,
'I'll be back,' he said.

I miss my father every day,
But all my mother does is cry and cry,
Until her eyes are dry.

Smreeti Rai (10)
Wavell Junior School, Catterick Garrison

The Joyful Streets

The street was joyful with lots of people smiling
The royal queen walking down the street proudly
Millions of people listening to musical instruments down the street
Listening to the music playing
People dancing, people singing
Birds singing, joining in the fun
The queen smiling proudly at everyone.

Shona Evans (8)
Wavell Junior School, Catterick Garrison

The Queen

The queen was walking through the hall
The ballroom was lit up in glitter
The food was bitter
The boys and girls were dancing
And the children were prancing
The beat was going
The trumpet was blowing.

Erin Grimes (8)
Wavell Junior School, Catterick Garrison

Autumn

Swirling, twirling leaves
Blow down
Bang and *whee, whizz* and *boom*
Fireworks fly in the sky
Trick or treat
Leave me something
Really good to eat.

Yazmin Puleston (8)
Wavell Junior School, Catterick Garrison

The Deep Blue Sea

The calm water slowly moving across the bright, bright blue sea
from far away,
The children splashing through the lovely bright blue sea,
The waves splashing upon the children,
The children dive into the deep blue sea,
The children all got out of the lovely blue sea
They lie down in the lovely sun.

Brooklyn Hicks-Williams (8)
Wavell Junior School, Catterick Garrison

Football

I love to play football,
It is my dream,
My mum and dad say
I am very keen,
I run very fast,
I run very slow,
I kick the ball into the goal!

Luke Hornby (8)
Wavell Junior School, Catterick Garrison

The Peacock

In autumn a peacock comes
Walking in the golden setting sun
Its beautiful amethyst eyes shine brightly.
Its feathers jewelled like a rainbow
In scarlet, ruby and amethyst
Amber gems walking on the rustling leaves
Its golden beak shining in the sun.

Sonu Pun (9)
Wavell Junior School, Catterick Garrison

Autumn

The leaves slowly twist and twirl down to the soft green grass
And the wind blows them up high into the sky.
Pumpkins lit up in the night ready to give people a fright
Then they will be blown out ready for the next light.
Boom, clash go the big loud fireworks
Shshsh go the blue ones.
Ssss go the pink ones.

Elisha Robertson (8)
Wavell Junior School, Catterick Garrison

Tigress

Tiger, tiger steadily strolling through your illuminous forest,
Your sapphire eyes shine in the dusky night,
Ruby, gold and amber leaves floating
And falling around your soft golden body,
The sapphire-blue sky magically highlights the horizon
With a golden glow of warmth.

Courtney Quinn, Shanice Decker, Demi Leigh Howard,
Ben Johnson, Rhys Bishop & Olivia Parish (9)
Wavell Junior School, Catterick Garrison

The Castle

The king is moving down the stairs
To the banqueting hall
In the hall people are gathering
The guards are outside guarding the castle
People are eating boars' heads and drinking wine
They are listening to the music.

Lewis Wilson (8)
Wavell Junior School, Catterick Garrison

The Autumn Fox

With his soft auburn fur,
He has amber eyes that shine in the dark,
Like purple and orange fire.
His teeth are sharp
And there are golden leaves
Falling gently to the ground.

Daniel Bratty (9)
Wavell Junior School, Catterick Garrison

Autumn

Autumn leaves
Swirling, twirling
Leaves fall down
Cold wind blowing in the sky
Children play in the leaves
Till the day is done.

Megan Dearden (8)
Wavell Junior School, Catterick Garrison

Autumn

Clear and mossy mist of red ruby leaves
falling from the trees
A steep hill of straight tall trees
with great green leaves, green dragon's scales
Ruby and amber leaves falling down
from the great brown trees.

Lenny Castel-Nuovo (9)
Wavell Junior School, Catterick Garrison

Autumn Fox

The fox gently walked across
the fiery autumn landscape
With its lovely jewelled ears
and its soft auburn fur
Its bushy red tail swishing everywhere.

Jezyka Galliers-Allison (9)
Wavell Junior School, Catterick Garrison

I Miss Dad

My heart is empty, my soul is hollow
Thinking of Dad I am weeping sorrow
Since Dad has gone our hearts are full of glum
My mother lonesome for her husband
I just want my dad to come home.

Martin Thackray (10)
Wavell Junior School, Catterick Garrison

The Hedgehog Of Autumn

As the hedgehog walked past the fiery smudged sun,
The leaves fell off the shimmering trees,
The slow spiky hedgehog walked through the golden,
scattered leaves,
It gently walked into a soft mist.

Eleanor West (9)
Wavell Junior School, Catterick Garrison

I Miss You Dad!

Dad I always cry.
I always hate thinking that you might die,
I hardly get any sleep,
I always need to have a peep,
To see if you are back.

Linnea Southam (11)
Wavell Junior School, Catterick Garrison

I Want To Go Home

I want to go home,
I want to go home,
I don't want to stay here
It stinks of sweat and hot heat coming into the tent
I try to hide the tears from the guys who are here.

Tina Platts (10)
Wavell Junior School, Catterick Garrison

Autumn

Blowing
Twirling cold
Crunchy howling
Whistling crispy
Swirling slithering.

Charlotte Lewis-Watkins (8)
Wavell Junior School, Catterick Garrison

The Bird

The fast, big bird was going along a fast river
Happy kids with smiling faces were jumping up and down
In the big park
It was going slower in and out of the tall buildings
Going down to its nest.

Bishnu Thapa (8)
Wavell Junior School, Catterick Garrison

The New King

People cheering, red, black,
Noise hollering, noise shouting
Joyful, mice sneaking, excited
New king, wedding day.

Sean Thompson (8)
Wavell Junior School, Catterick Garrison

Untitled

Trees old and new
Grew, grew, grew
Standing in dirty mud
Roots hold the trees up.

Jessica Sinclair (7)
Wavell Junior School, Catterick Garrison

The Love Child

My heart is broken.
I know people care.
About their loved ones in the war.
Every day I make up a prayer.

I am lonesome for my dad.
Out in that land.
When is he back?
I miss his loving hand.

Arran MacMillan (10)
Wavell Junior School, Catterick Garrison

Young Writers Information

We hope you have enjoyed reading this book - and that you will continue to enjoy it in the coming years.

If you like reading and writing poetry drop us a line, or give us a call, and we'll send you a free information pack.

Alternatively if you would like to order further copies of this book or any of our other titles, then please give us a call or log onto our website at www.youngwriters.co.uk.

Young Writers Information
Remus House
Coltsfoot Drive
Peterborough
PE2 9JX
(01733) 890066